POSH

EGGS

Over 70 recipes for
wonderful eggy things

Recipes by Lucy O'Reilly
Photography by Louise Hagger

quadrille

Publishing Director: Sarah Lavelle
Creative Director: Helen Lewis
Copy Editor: Kate Wanwimolruk
Series Designer: Gemma Hayden
Designer: Katherine Keeble
Photography and Prop Styling: Louise Hagger
Recipe Writer and Food Styling: Lucy O'Reilly
Recipes on Pages 61 and 122: Emily Kydd
Production Controller: Tom Moore
Production Director: Vincent Smith

First published in 2016 by
Quadrille Publishing Limited
Pentagon House
52–54 Southwark Street
London SE1 1UN
www.quadrille.co.uk

Quadrille is an imprint of Hardie Grant
www.hardiegrant.com.au

Cataloguing in Publication Data: a catalogue record for this
book is available from the British Library.

ISBN: 978 1 84949 788 6   33614057805441

Printed in China

CONTENTS

— 🍴 ★ 🍴 —

INTRODUCTION

Eggs, so often overlooked or taken for granted, are one of the most beautiful, magical ingredients that nature has ever provided. They are satisfying to hold, their shells smooth and oval. Speckled, freckled and coloured, we have a choice of hen, quail, duck, goose, ostrich, even gull. Each unique in colour, size and flavour and cleverly packaged so that the delicate contents are protected within a perfect porous vessel. It is what lies within that provides us with a rich nutritious source of culinary experiment. Often lost, tucked amongst the other ingredients of a Full English breakfast and neglected until the weekend, isn't it about time we brought that box of eggs to the forefront of our cooking staples and celebrated this humble food?

An egg contains two ingredients: a yolk and a white. They have different properties and can be used together or separately. The yolk can be emulsified together with other ingredients to produce creamy mayonnaise, custard and hollandaise. The white can be whipped into a pillowy meringue, a foamy cocktail or a soufflé. Together, the two can add flavour, richness and lightness to cakes, omelettes, quiches and mousse. There are endless possibilities for such a modest ingredient.

Can there be anything more pleasing than the tap-tap and crack that heralds the morning boiled egg? Then you open its lid to dunk hot buttered toast into the golden yolk within. Even fussy toddlers will happily tuck into a runny egg with fat Marmite soldiers. And is there any meal that cannot be elevated by the addition of an egg on top? Eggs can perform so much other culinary magic, however. Their neutral, rich flavour provides an ideal background for a huge array of ingredients, both savoury and sweet. Combine with mustard, salty bacon, fresh herbs, mature cheddar, anchovies, spiced cayenne, smoked fish, celery salt, bitter salad leaves and warm lentils. And that's just the beginning… There's also lemon, cream, sharp apples, chocolate and cinnamon to consider.

Always buy good-quality free-range eggs. A caged chicken lives a miserable life and this is reflected in the quality of the egg it produces. You will be rewarded with a good healthy egg, a pert yolk the colour of the sunset, a strong gelatinous white and a delicious taste. Look out particularly for Burford Browns or Old Cotswold Legbar.

Eggs should be as fresh as possible for frying, whisking and poaching; slightly older eggs are best for boiling and peeling. To test, place your egg in a glass of water. A fresh egg will sink and assume a horizontal position, a slightly older egg will tilt slightly and an old egg will float vertically (as carbon monoxide is slowly released into the air sac).

The phrase 'You can't even boil an egg' is shorthand for 'You can't cook anything, no matter how simple'. However, there is need for careful cooking and basic knowledge to cook an egg perfectly. Get it right, and an egg will make you proud.

From providing reassuringly humble treats to something very, very posh, without the mighty egg, our culinary lives would be infinitely poorer.

COOKING WITH

★

EGGS

Boiling
You can boil eggs in cold or boiling water. Either way, accurate timing is essential.

For a soft-boiled egg, my preferred method is to place a small pan of water on the hob and bring to the boil. Carefully lower in your eggs, reduce to a simmer and leave for exactly 6 minutes before removing and quickly transferring to an egg cup.

For a hard-boiled egg, cook for 10 minutes, then immediately plunge into a bowl of iced water. This will stop the cooking process and make removing the shell easier.

Poaching
I admit to a problem with poaching eggs. In my early days as a food stylist, I would stay up late the night before a shoot creating the perfect poached egg, discarding many along the way.

For the perfect teardrop shape, use only the freshest eggs. Crack one egg into a cup. Use a wide pan filled 5cm deep with water, and bring to a simmer. Add a teaspoon of vinegar, to help solidify the white, and stir to create a good swirl with the end of a spoon. Once it slows, add the egg into the centre and leave to poach for 3 minutes or until the white has just set, while the yolk remains runny. Lift out with a slotted spoon.

Scrambling
So often overcooked, rubbery, weeping eggs are the stuff of hotel breakfast nightmares.

For a creamy, velvety result, whisk the eggs together in a bowl with a splash of cream or milk and a pinch of salt and pepper. Melt a knob of butter in a pan over a medium heat, pour in the eggs and draw a wooden spoon slowly through to allow large curds to form. Remove from the heat whilst there is still a spoonful of runniness and quickly pile onto hot buttered toast.

Frying
The temperature at which you fry your eggs will determine the texture and amount of fat absorbed. A high heat results in a crispy frilly edge and a bubbly white. A lower temperature ensures a silky, moist egg.

Lightly oil a non-stick pan and warm through. Carefully crack a fresh egg into the pan and leave to cook for 2–3 minutes, or until the white has set and the yolk is still runny (or to your liking). 'Sunny-side up' means cooked on just one side, while 'over easy' describes frying on both sides so that the yolk remains runny in the centre.

Omelette

An omelette, a golden wobbly plate of loveliness, should never be overcooked. There should be a degree of runniness, *baveuse*, as the French call it.

Blend 2–3 eggs together in a bowl with a pinch of salt and pepper. Place a medium pan (18cm/7 inches across the base is perfect) over a medium-high heat with a dash of oil. Add the eggs, swirl to coat the base and then leave for 10 seconds. Begin drawing in the sides with a wooden spoon, tilting the pan so that the runny egg fills the gap. When there is a small amount of liquid left on the surface, carefully flip one side over to meet the other and wiggle onto a plate.

Notes on the recipes

Please note that all the recipes in this book use medium eggs unless otherwise stated.

If you keep your eggs in the fridge, always bring them up to room temperature half an hour or so before cooking.

BREAKFAST

★

EGGS

BREAKFAST

★

CUPS

A Full English breakfast baked into a muffin. Portable and
a near-perfect combination of ingredients.

 MAKES 12

 TAKES 40 minutes

12 good-quality cocktail sausages
12 cherry tomatoes, halved
drizzle of olive oil
6–12 slices white bread
   (depending on size)
12 slices smoked streaky bacon
40g/1½oz finely grated Cheddar
squeeze of tomato ketchup
12 eggs
few chopped chives
salt and freshly ground
   black pepper

Preheat the oven to 200°C/400°F/gas 6. Tumble the
sausages and cherry tomatoes into a lipped baking
tray. Drizzle over a little oil and roll the sausages
and tomatoes in it until well coated, then season
the tomatoes. Cook in the oven for 12 minutes,
until the sausages are cooked through.

Toast the bread and use a 6cm/2½ inch round
pastry cutter to stamp out 12 rounds, discarding
the crusts.

Grease a 12-hole muffin tin well with oil and press
a piece of toast into the base of each hole. Line
the inside edge with a slice of bacon and fill
with some grated cheese, a cherry tomato half,
a cocktail sausage, and a squeeze of ketchup.
Crack an egg into each and finish with some
chives and seasoning.

Bake in the oven for 20 minutes. Run a knife
around the edges to release before removing,
and serve warm.

EGGY CRUMPETS

Here is the perfect breakfast to feed a houseful. You can make the beans the day before then simply reheat and fry your crumpets as and when sleepyheads appear.

 SERVES 4

 TAKES 35 minutes

1 tbsp olive oil, plus extra,
  for frying
1 red onion, finely chopped
85g/3oz smoked streaky bacon,
  chopped
400g/14oz tin chopped tomatoes
1 tbsp dark muscovado sugar
1 tbsp red wine vinegar
400g/14oz tin haricot beans,
  drained and rinsed
dash of hot chilli sauce (optional)
handful chopped flat-leaf
  parsley leaves
For the eggy crumpets
4 eggs
1 tbsp harissa (optional)
8 crumpets
good knob of butter
salt and freshly ground
  black pepper

Heat the oil in a pan, add the onion and bacon and fry over medium heat for 5 minutes, stirring now and then. Add the tomatoes, sugar, vinegar and 100ml/3½fl oz water, and simmer for 20 minutes. Now stir in the drained beans and continue to simmer for a few more minutes to warm the beans through. Add a dash of hot sauce if you like, and the chopped parsley.

Whisk two of the eggs, the harissa and seasoning in a shallow bowl. Add 4 of the crumpets and immerse on both sides; the crumpet will soak up the eggs like a sponge. Heat half the butter and a drizzle of oil in a pan, add the four egg-soaked crumpets and fry for around 2 minutes each side over a medium heat, until golden and crisp. Remove and keep warm while you repeat with the remaining eggs and crumpets. Spoon the bacon beans on top to serve.

SCRAMBLED EGGS WITH
★
FINNAN HADDIE

Finnan haddie is a cold-smoked haddock. Its smoky, salty
flavour works undeniably well with creamy scrambled eggs.

 SERVES 2

 TAKES 15 minutes

200g/7oz Finnan haddie or other
smoked haddock fillet
350ml/11½fl oz full-fat (whole)
milk
4 eggs
1 tbsp chopped chives and dill
good knob of butter, for frying
20g/¾oz finely grated Parmesan
2 slices wholegrain (whole-wheat)
bread, toasted and buttered
lemon wedges, to serve
freshly ground black pepper

Put the haddock into a small pan and cover with
the milk. Bring to a simmer, cook for 2 minutes
then remove from the heat and leave the fish
to steep for 5 minutes, or until cooked through.
Remove with a slotted spoon and flake into large
pieces, discarding the skin and any bones. Reserve
50ml/3½ tbsp of the milk and leave to cool.

Whisk the eggs in a bowl with the reserved milk,
half the herbs and a little pepper. Melt the butter
in a frying pan. Add the eggs and cook gently over
low heat, scrambling with a wooden spoon. When
the eggs are half cooked, fold though the flaked
haddock, Parmesan and the remaining herbs to
warm through. Spoon onto the buttered toast and
serve with lemon wedges to squeeze over.

QUESADILLA

Quesadillas are a brilliant way to get kids to eat a good breakfast. Omit the harissa and they'll love these handheld cheesy triangles. They're a great way to use up leftovers, too.

SERVES 2–4

TAKES 20 minutes

1 large ripe avocado
½ tsp ground cumin
juice of ½ lime
2 spring onions (scallions),
   finely sliced
80g/3oz cherry tomatoes,
   chopped
3 eggs
1 tbsp soured cream or
   crème fraîche
1½ tsp harissa
knob of butter
2 tbsp finely chopped
   coriander (cilantro) leaves
4 soft white wraps
80g/3oz grated Cheddar
salt and freshly ground
   black pepper

Halve the avocado, remove the stone and scoop out the flesh into a bowl. Use a fork to roughly mash in the cumin, lime juice and some seasoning. Fold through the spring onions (scallions) and tomatoes, and set aside.

Whisk the eggs in a bowl with the soured cream, harissa and seasoning. Melt the butter in a frying pan over medium heat. Add the eggs and gently scramble using a wooden spoon, then gently fold through the chopped coriander (cilantro).

Take one wrap and spread half the avocado mixture over evenly. Spoon over half the eggs and finish with half the grated Cheddar. Top with another wrap, pressing down a little to help seal. Repeat with the remaining ingredients.

Place a dry griddle or frying pan over medium heat. Cook one quesadilla at a time for 3 minutes, carefully flipping over with a fish slice onto the other side for a further 2–3 minutes, or until crisp and melted. Remove and fry the remaining quesadilla. Slice and serve while warm.

★

KEDGEREE

Kedgeree is perfect as fuel to start off the day, not to
mention a fantastic brunch dish. It's also full of protein
with a hint of spice – comfort in a bowl.

  SERVES 4

TAKES 20 minutes

1 tbsp olive oil
30g/1oz butter
1 large onion,
   finely chopped
5 cardamom pods, crushed
1 tbsp curry powder
1 green chilli pepper, deseeded
   and chopped
300g/10½oz basmati rice, rinsed
   under cold water
1 bay leaf
4 eggs
100g/3½oz frozen peas
320g/11oz smoked mackerel
2 tbsp double (heavy) cream
1 lemon, cut into wedges
bunch coriander (cilantro)
   leaves, chopped
salt and freshly ground
   black pepper

Heat the oil and and melt the butter in a pan over
low heat. Add the onion and cook for 5 minutes,
until softened. Increase the heat to medium, add
the spices and chilli, and cook for a further minute.
Tip the rice into the pan and stir to coat with the
buttery, spiced onion. Add the bay leaf and season,
then pour in 600ml/20fl oz cold water. Bring to the
boil over high heat, reduce the heat to low, cover
and simmer for 12 minutes, until the rice is cooked.

Meanwhile, bring a small pan of water to the boil,
lower in your eggs and simmer over a low heat for
6 minutes. Add the peas to the pan, and cook for a
further minute. Drain both the peas and the eggs.
Run the eggs briefly under cold water, then peel.

Warm the mackerel through in the microwave,
covered, for about 1 minute (on medium) or in a
low oven (about 125°C/255°F/gas ½) for 8 minutes.
Remove and discard the skin and flake the flesh.

Fold the cream through the rice, squeeze over
some lemon juice, then fork through the mackerel,
peas and coriander (cilantro). Slice the boiled eggs
and arrange over the top of the rice. Serve with
extra lemon wedges on the side.

BREAKFAST-STUFFED
★
CROISSANTS

The secret to good scrambled eggs is butter, cream and a gentle heat. The eggs will continue to cook in the heat of the pan so remove from the hob while there is still a spoonful of runniness.

 SERVES 2

 TAKES 15 minutes

6 rashers streaky bacon
1 tbsp maple syrup
pinch of cayenne pepper
2 buttery croissants
good knob of butter
4 eggs, lightly beaten
2 tbsp double (heavy) cream
handful of chives, snipped

Preheat the oven to 180°C/350°F/gas 4. Toss the streaky bacon in the maple syrup and cayenne. Line a baking tray with baking parchment, lay the bacon over the top and pop into the oven for 20 minutes, turning halfway, until crisp. At the halfway mark, put the croissants in the oven to warm through.

Meanwhile, melt the butter in a frying pan over medium heat. Whisk the eggs, cream, chives and some seasoning together in a bowl. Pour into the pan and cook, gently moving a wooden spoon backwards and forwards through the eggs to scramble. When there is still a little runny egg remaining, immediately remove from the heat.

Split the croissants and stuff with the maple bacon and a generous spoonful of the creamy scrambled eggs. Serve immediately.

MEXICAN
★
ROSTADA

This Mexican-inspired 'tostada' on a rösti base is sure to kick-start your day. Sriracha sauce adds a fiery sweetness.

 SERVES 2

 TAKES 25 minutes

For the rostada
350g/12½oz (about 2 medium-
   sized) Desiree potatoes
1 small red onion
2 tbsp plain (all-purpose) flour
½ tsp smoked paprika
½ tsp salt
2 spring onions (scallions), diced
2 tbsp chopped coriander
   (cilantro) leaves
1 egg, lightly beaten
vegetable oil, for shallow frying
salt and black pepper
To serve
2 eggs
1 ripe avocado
juice of ½ lime
½ green chilli pepper, deseeded
   and finely sliced
soured cream
pinch smoked paprika
a few coriander (cilantro) and
   mint leaves
Sriracha hot sauce

Coarsely grate the potatoes and onion, wrap in a clean tea towel or J-cloth and squeeze out as much liquid as you can. Put in a bowl and stir through the flour, paprika, salt, spring onions (scallions), coriander (cilantro) and egg. Mix well.

Heat enough oil to cover the base of your pan by about 1cm/½ inch over medium heat. Add half the rostada mixture, spooning it evenly across the pan. Fry for 3 minutes, or until golden brown, then flip over and fry the other side for a further 3 minutes until golden, crisp and cooked through. Remove the rostada with a slotted spoon and drain on kitchen paper. Repeat with the remaining mixture.

Drain the oil from the pan and put back over medium heat. Crack your eggs in and fry until the white has set but the yolk remains runny, for about 3 minutes.

Meanwhile, peel and slice the avocado and squeeze over the lime. Top each rostada with a fried egg, the avocado, chilli, a spoonful of soured cream, a sprinkling of paprika, the herbs and a drizzle of hot sauce.

TURKISH

★

MENEMEN

A simple yet gutsy dish of baked eggs. Allow your guests to
spoon this straight from the pan, with warmed flatbreads
for mopping and dipping. If you like, try it topped with
fried chorizo morsels.

 SERVES 4

 TAKES 30 minutes

2 tbsp olive oil
1 onion, finely sliced
1 tsp fennel seeds
½ tsp cumin seeds
1 large green chilli pepper,
    deseeded and chopped
2 red and 2 yellow (or green) bell
    peppers, deseeded and
    finely sliced
400g/14oz tin chopped tomatoes
4 eggs
pinch of cayenne
handful coriander (cilantro) and
    mint leaves, chopped
flatbreads, warmed, to serve
salt and freshly ground
    black pepper
For the garlic yoghurt
1 large garlic clove, crushed
squeeze of lemon juice
1 tbsp extra virgin olive oil
140g/5oz Greek yoghurt

Heat the oil in a large pan. Add the onion and cook
slowly over low heat for 8 minutes, until soft and
golden. Stir through the fennel and cumin seeds,
and chilli, and cook for a further minute. Add the
peppers, cook for 2–3 more minutes, then pour
over the chopped tomatoes and a splash of water.
Season well and allow the sauce to bubble for
5 minutes, until aromatic and slightly thickened.

Make shallow depressions in the sauce and crack
in your eggs. Cook over low heat for around 15
minutes until the whites have set but yolks are
still runny.

Meanwhile, combine the garlic, lemon and extra
virgin olive oil with the yoghurt in a bowl and
season to taste.

Sprinkle the eggs with the cayenne, seasoning and
the chopped herbs. Serve directly out of the pan
at the table with the cooling garlicky yoghurt and
warm flatbreads.

ITALIAN

★

SAUSAGE & EGG

This is a serious sandwich. *Salciccia*, a coarse crumbly pork and fennel sausage, is sold in good Italian delis and is quite wonderful when paired with a runny egg.

 SERVES 2

TAKES 20 minutes
plus chilling

255g/9oz Salciccia or fennel
   and pork sausages
2 eggs, plus a little extra
   beaten egg
1 tbsp olive oil
1 small ciabatta, split in half
   lengthways then halved
drizzle of extra virgin olive oil
70g/2½oz Taleggio or provolone
   cheese, thinly sliced
4 thin slices prosciutto
few Parmesan shavings
few basil leaves

Squeeze the sausage from its skin into a bowl, breaking it up as you go. Add a little beaten egg to help the mixture bind. Shape into two patties about 2.5cm/1 inch thick and chill for 20 minutes.

Heat the oil in a frying pan, add the patties and fry for 3–4 minutes each side, or until cooked through and golden. Remove and keep warm.

Preheat the grill to medium-high. Drizzle the cut sides of the ciabatta with oil and lightly toast under the grill. Remove the two 'tops' of the ciabatta, set aside, and lay the cheese on the bottom halves. Add the prosciutto to the tray. Put back under the grill for 2 minutes or until the cheese is melted and the ham crisp.

Heat a pan over medium heat and crack in the eggs. Fry for 2 minutes, then flip and cook the other side for a further minute (so the yolks remain runny).

To assemble, put a piece of cheesy bread on each plate. Top with a sausage patty and an egg. Add 2 pieces of crisp prosciutto, a few Parmesan shavings, some basil leaves and a final drizzle of extra virgin olive oil. Top with the remaining ciabatta half.

CRISP FRIED EGG &

★

CHORIZO BAP

A fried egg with a golden bottom and frilly edge. With every blissful bite you'll have crisp white, some warm, runny yolk and spicy, salty chorizo.

 SERVES 2

 TAKES 15 minutes

1 ripe avocado
squeeze of lemon
¼ red chilli pepper, deseeded and
    finely diced
130g/4½oz chorizo picante, sliced
    about 5mm/¼ inch thick on an
    angle
2 brioche buns, split
1 tbsp rapeseed oil
2 eggs
handful rocket
salt and freshly ground
    black pepper

Peel the avocado and use a fork to roughly mash the flesh in a bowl with a squeeze of lemon, the chilli and some seasoning. There should still be some chunks of avocado.

Preheat a griddle pan. When hot, add the chorizo slices and cook for 1–2 minutes each side, until heated through and charred. Griddle the buns on the cut side for 30 seconds, until charred.

Heat the oil in a frying pan over high heat. Crack in the eggs; they should almost explode in the hot oil, with the whites puffing up around the yolks. Fry for 2 minutes or until the whites are cooked with crispy bottoms and lacy edges – the yolks should still be runny.

Spread the bun bases with smashed avocado and top with a lacy fried egg, the chorizo and a handful of peppery rocket.

EGGS

★

BENEDICT

This classic poached egg recipe is made 'posh' with ham hock, complementing the rich, buttery hollandaise.

 SERVES 2

 TAKES 30 minutes

good knob of butter
1 tbsp demerara sugar
200g/7oz smoked ham hock, torn, or thickly sliced ham
good pinch of cayenne pepper
4 whole eggs
2 slices toasted sourdough
1 tbsp pumpkin seeds
salt and freshly ground black pepper
For the hollandaise sauce
100g/3½oz butter
2 egg yolks
1 tsp lemon juice plus extra if needed
½ tsp English mustard

Melt the butter in a small pan. In a bowl set over pan of simmering water, or in a food processor, mix the egg yolks, lemon juice and mustard. Gradually spoon in tiny drops of the warm melted butter (leave the white solids behind in the pan), whisking (or pulsing if using a food processor) all the time. Season and loosen the mixture with a little more lemon juice if needed. Keep warm.

Melt a knob of butter in a frying pan over a medium heat, add the sugar and allow to dissolve. Add the ham, sprinkle over the cayenne and fry for 4 minutes or until glazed, turning every now and then.

Put enough water to come up to 5cm/2 inches into a large pan and bring to the boil over high heat. Reduce the heat down to a shudder. In turn, crack each egg into a teacup and carefully slide it into the water, on separate sides of the pan. Cook for 3 minutes until the white has set. Remove using a slotted spoon and briefly drain on kitchen paper.

Top the toasts with the glazed ham, poached eggs and then spoon the warm hollandaise over the top. Finish with some cracked black pepper and the pumpkin seeds.

★

PANCAKES WITH CHORIZO

Breakfast pancakes are so versatile. For sweet pancakes,
leave out the savoury flavourings and add a spoonful of
sugar and handful of blueberries to the batter.

 SERVES 4

TAKES 20 minutes

155g/5½oz chorizo, roughly
  chopped
1 tbsp oregano leaves
200g/7oz self-raising flour
1 tsp baking powder
¼ tsp salt
pinch of freshly ground black
  pepper
5 large eggs
240ml/8fl oz full-fat (whole) milk
100g/3½oz coarsely grated
  halloumi
olive oil, for frying

Heat a frying pan over medium heat and fry the
chorizo until it starts to crisp up and release its
oils. Stir in the oregano. Remove the chorizo with
a slotted spoon, reserving the pan oils for drizzling,
and set aside to cool. Wipe the pan for use later.

Sift the flour, baking powder, salt and pepper into
a large bowl. Make a well in the middle, whisk 1 egg
and the milk in a jug and pour half the mixture into
the well. Stir with a wooden spoon, drawing in the
flour, then add the remaining milk. Fold through the
grated halloumi and two-thirds of the chorizo.

Heat a little oil in a non-stick frying pan over
medium heat. Add 3 heaped tablespoons of the
mixture, shape into rounds and fry for 2–3 minutes
or until large bubbles appear on the surface. Flip
and continue to fry until golden and cooked
through. Repeat with the remaining batter and oil,
keeping each batch loosely covered with foil.

Heat a little oil in the pan you used to cook the
chorizo and crack in the remaining eggs. Fry for
2 minutes over medium heat.

To serve, stack three pancakes on top of one
another. Top with a fried egg and spoon over the
reserved chorizo and its oil, and serve.

LUNCH

★

EGGS

GREEN

★

SHAKSHUKA

There are many variations on an Israeli shakshuka. Here,
the eggs are baked within a nest of garlicky greens, sharp
tangy feta and olives. If you come across purple kale it
makes a pretty addition.

 SERVES 2

 TAKES 25 minutes

1 tbsp olive oil
1 onion, finely chopped
1 garlic clove, finely chopped
½ tsp ground cumin
½ tsp ground coriander
55g/2oz mixed shredded greens
   such as kale or chard (any thick
   stems removed)
110g/4oz baby spinach leaves
3 tbsp double (heavy) cream
1 tbsp lemon juice
40g/1½oz black and green pitted
   olives, roughly chopped
2 eggs
55g/2oz feta
handful chopped parsley leaves
small handful dill sprigs
½ red chilli pepper, finely sliced
pinch of sumac (optional)
salt and freshly ground
   black pepper

Heat the oil in a small frying pan, add the onion
and cook for 5 minutes over a low heat until
softened. Stir through the garlic and spices, and
continue to cook for a couple of minutes. Fold
through the shredded greens and season well.
Cover and cook for 1 minute, then uncover and
continue to cook for a further 3 minutes. Add the
baby spinach, folding through to wilt the leaves.

Stir in the cream, lemon juice and olives. Make
two depressions in the vegetables and crack your
eggs into these. Crumble over the feta and scatter
with the herbs and chilli. Season the eggs with the
sumac and salt and pepper, then cook gently for 12
minutes, or until the egg whites have set. Serve in
the pan at the table.

PARMESAN CUSTARDS &
★
CRISPY BACON

These are sinful savoury baked custards served with crisp,
smoked streaky bacon for dipping. Anchovy toasts would
also be a wonderful addition.

 SERVES 4

 TAKES 50 minutes
plus infusing

150ml/5fl oz double (heavy) cream
150ml/5fl oz milk
55g/2oz finely grated Parmesan
    plus 4 tablespoons for sprinkling
2 large egg yolks
pinch of salt
½ tsp mustard powder
8 rashers smoked streaky bacon,
    to serve

Heat the cream, milk and Parmesan in a small
saucepan over low heat, stirring every now and
then, until a few bubbles appear at the edges.
Remove from the heat, cover and set aside for 30
minutes to allow the flavours to infuse. Preheat the
oven to 150°C/300°F/gas 2.

Whisk the egg yolks in a bowl with the salt and
mustard powder. Slowly pour in the Parmesan
cream, whisking well as you do so. Divide the
mixture between four small 100ml/3½fl oz ramekins
and arrange in a roasting tray. Carefully pour just-
boiled water into the tin to reach two-thirds up
the sides of the ramekins. Cook in the oven for 30
minutes. Sprinkle each with a tablespoon of grated
Parmesan then return to the oven for a further 10
minutes. Remove from the oven and leave in the
water bath for 5 minutes.

Preheat the grill to medium-high. Spread the bacon
rashers out on a baking tray and grill for 3 minutes,
turning once until crisp. Serve the custards whilst
still warm with the crispy bacon for dipping.

SALAD

★

LYONNAISE

A simple French salad of bitter leaves, salty bacon and vinegar dressing, with a runny poached egg nestled at its centre. Use really fresh eggs for a perfect poach.

  SERVES 2

TAKES 15 minutes

1 head frisée lettuce or other
　　bitter leaves
2 eggs
1 tbsp extra virgin olive oil
100g/3½oz smoked streaky bacon,
　　sliced into lardons
1 shallot, finely diced
1 tbsp red wine vinegar
1 tsp Dijon mustard
salt and freshly ground
　　black pepper

Remove and discard the tough outer leaves from the lettuce. Rinse and pat the inner leaves dry with kitchen paper, separate into bite-sized pieces and set aside in a bowl.

To poach the eggs, put about 5cm/2 inches water into a pan, bring to the boil over a high heat then reduce the heat right down to a shudder. Crack each egg into a teacup and gently slide them into the water, at separate sides of the pan. Cook for 3 minutes and then remove with a slotted spoon and drain briefly on kitchen paper.

Meanwhile, heat the oil in a frying pan over medium heat. Add the bacon and fry until crisp. Remove with a slotted spoon and set aside. Add the shallot to the pan and fry for 30 seconds. Stir in the vinegar and mustard, return the bacon to the pan and season with salt and pepper. Spoon the warm dressing over the salad leaves and toss to coat. Divide the salad between two plates and top with the softly poached eggs and a pinch of cracked black pepper.

MINI POTATO &

★

CHORIZO TORTILLA

A perfect tortilla should be crispy and golden around the
edges and slightly runny in the very centre.

 SERVES 2

 TAKES 25 minutes

250g/9oz Charlotte or other small
    waxy potatoes
3 tbsp olive oil plus extra
    for greasing
½ onion, finely sliced
40g/1½oz finely sliced chorizo
3 eggs, beaten
small handful flat-leaf parsley
    leaves, finely chopped
salt and freshly ground
    black pepper

Very finely slice the potatoes on a mandoline or
with a sharp knife. Heat the oil in a frying pan over
medium heat, add the potato and onion and fry
for 10 minutes, tossing the pan every now and then.
Add the chorizo and continue to cook for 3 more
minutes, until the potatoes are golden and tender.
Remove from the heat and allow to cool briefly.

Whisk the eggs in a large bowl and season well. Tip
the potato and onion into the bowl, along with the
chopped parsley, and gently mix.

Place two small 12cm/5 inch greased non-stick
frying pans over medium-high heat. Add half of
the mixture to each pan (the photograph, opposite,
shows the mixture at this stage). Cook for 4
minutes, or until nicely golden, loosen the sides
with a fish slice, then carefully flip the tortilla,
and brown on the other side for 2 more minutes.
Turn out onto serving plates and leave to sit for 5
minutes before eating.

TRUFFLES &

★

DUCK EGG

Duck eggs are larger and arguably better in flavour than most commercial hen's eggs. Simply fry and serve them with shavings of truffle or drizzled in melted butter.

 SERVES 2

 TAKES 10 minutes

2 thick slices sourdough or
   country-style bread
extra virgin olive oil or truffle oil,
   to drizzle
1 garlic clove, halved
1 tbsp duck fat or rapeseed oil
2 duck eggs
few small fresh thyme sprigs
black summer truffle, as much as
   you dare, to serve
salt and freshly ground
   black pepper

Preheat the grill. Place the bread on a baking tray, drizzle with the oil and some seasoning and toast for 1–2 minutes on each side, until golden. Rub the toasts with the cut side of a garlic clove.

Meanwhile, heat the duck fat or oil in a frying pan. Crack the eggs into the pan, season and gently fry over medium heat for 3 minutes, or until the whites are set and the yolks are to your liking. Add the thyme leaves towards the end of cooking.

Place the toasts on your plates and top with the fried eggs. Finish with a drizzle of oil and a scattering of finely shaved truffle.

SMOKED HADDOCK
★
SCOTCH EGGS

Egg and smoked fish complement each other perfectly,
especially when packaged up as a crisp, golden Scotch egg.

 MAKES 4

 TAKES 40 minutes
plus chilling

5 eggs plus 1 egg white
150g/5½oz skinless cod fillet,
   roughly chopped
150g/5½oz skinless smoked
   haddock fillet, chopped
1 tbsp chopped tarragon leaves
1 tbsp chopped flat-leaf
   parsley leaves
1 tbsp chopped capers
grated zest of 1 lemon
55g/2oz plain (all-purpose) flour,
   seasoned with salt and pepper
70g/2½oz fine polenta
vegetable oil, for deep-frying
tartare sauce, to serve
salt and freshly ground
   black pepper

Bring a pan of water to the boil. Carefully lower in 4 eggs and boil for 6 minutes. Remove the eggs with a slotted spoon, plunge into a bowl of iced water to cool quickly, then carefully peel them.

Blitz the cod, egg white and seasoning to a purée in a food processor. Add the haddock, and pulse to mix through. Transfer to a bowl and stir through the chopped herbs, capers, lemon zest and seasoning.

Divide into four portions (about 85g/3oz), and flatten each into a 13cm/5 inch circle. Working with one portion and one egg at a time, dust the egg in the flour and place in the centre of the fish mixture. Use your hands to mould the mixture up and around, encasing the egg completely, patching where needed. Place on a plate lined with kitchen paper and chill for 20 minutes.

In a bowl, lightly beat the remaining egg. Put the remaining seasoned flour and polenta in two separate shallow bowls. Dust each encased egg first in the flour, then in the egg and finally the polenta.

Heat the oil in a large, deep-sided pan to 180°C/350°F/gas 4 on a thermometer (or test the temperature by dropping in a cube of bread – it will turn golden in 60 seconds when the oil is ready). Deep-fry two eggs at a time for 8 minutes, until crisp and golden. Remove with a slotted spoon and briefly drain on kitchen paper. Serve warm with creamy tartare sauce.

TURKISH

★

EGGS

A glorious yet simple dish of garlicky, herb-infused yoghurt adorned with a poached egg and spiced butter. Use the freshest eggs for a perfect poach.

 SERVES 4

 TAKES 10 minutes

400g/14oz Greek yoghurt, at room
    temperature
zest and juice of 1 lemon
2 garlic cloves, crushed
1½ tsp tahini
4 eggs
55g/2oz butter
¼ tsp smoked paprika
¼ tsp Aleppo chilli flakes (red
    pepper flakes)
few small mint and coriander
    (cilantro) leaves, to serve
warmed pita breads, to serve
salt and freshly ground
    black pepper

Spoon the yoghurt into a bowl and stir through the lemon zest and juice, garlic and tahini. Season with salt and pepper.

To poach your eggs, put enough water in a pan to come up to about 5cm/2 inches, and bring to the boil over high heat. Reduce the heat right down to a shudder. In turn, crack each egg into a teacup and slide it into the water, at separate sides of the pan. Cook for 3 minutes until the white has just set.

Meanwhile, melt the butter in a small pan. Add the paprika and chilli and cook for 2 minutes, until the butter smells spicy.

Remove the eggs from the water with a slotted spoon and drain briefly on kitchen paper.

Spoon the yoghurt between four small bowls. Top each with a poached egg, pour over the warm spiced butter and finish with a scattering of herbs. Serve with warm pitas for dunking.

JAPANESE
★
OYAKODON

Here is a classic form of the Japanese rice bowl, *donburi*,
which has a curious cooking method. The name *oyako*
means 'parent and child': the chicken and egg.

SERVES 2

TAKES 30 minutes

120g/4¼oz sushi or short-grain
   rice, rinsed until the water
   runs clear
3½ tbsp mirin
3 tbsp soy sauce
4 tbsp dashi or vegetable stock
3 skinless boneless chicken thighs
   (about 230g/8oz total), trimmed
   of excess fat and cut into
   2.5cm/1 inch cubes
1 small onion, sliced
3 eggs, very lightly beaten
For the garnish
1 spring onion (scallion), finely
   shredded
few coriander (cilantro) leaves
¼ nori sheet, crumbled

Cook the rice according to packet instructions.

Put a small 17cm/7 inch pan over medium heat. Pour
in the mirin, soy sauce and dashi, and bring to the
boil. Add the chicken and onion, bring back up to the
boil then simmer for 5 minutes, stirring occasionally.

Carefully, slowly and evenly pour most the beaten
eggs over the top of the chicken and onion. Cover
with a lid and gently simmer for 1 minute 30 seconds.
Pour over the remaining egg, recover and cook for
a further 30 seconds. Take off the heat and leave to
rest for 1 minute.

Divide the rice between serving bowls, spoon the
chicken and eggs over the top with any liquid from
pan, and garnish with the spring onion (scallion),
coriander (cilantro) leaves and a little crumbled nori.

MONTE

★

CRISTO

A variation on the French *croque monsieur*, here the bread
is stuffed with Spanish ham and manchego, fried in an egg
batter and served with membrillo (quince paste).

 SERVES 4

 TAKES 15 minutes

2 tbsp Dijon mustard
100g/3½oz mayonnaise (see page
  88 for home-made)
8 slices country-style bread
  or sourdough
8 thin slices Serrano ham
130g/4½oz manchego, rind
  removed and thinly sliced
3 eggs
25g/1oz butter
membrillo (quince paste), to serve
salt and freshly ground
  black pepper

In a bowl, combine the mustard and mayonnaise
and spread onto the slices of bread. Top half the
slices with the ham and manchego, sandwich
together with the remaining bread slices and press
down a little to seal.

Beat the eggs in a shallow bowl and season with
salt and pepper. Soak both sides of each sandwich
well in the eggs.

Melt half the butter in a frying pan over medium
heat. Transfer half the eggy sandwiches to the
hot pan and fry for 2–3 minutes on each side
until golden, crisp and melted. Repeat with the
remaining butter and sandwiches. Serve hot with
the membrillo alongside.

BACON SALAD WITH
★
BEETROOT & QUAIL EGGS

Bacon and eggs are a dream team in salads as well
as at breakfast time, and this is a positively healthy way
of eating both!

 SERVES 4

 TAKES 20 minutes

10 quail eggs
150g/5½oz fresh peas
drizzle of olive oil
6 rashers streaky bacon
200g/7oz packet ready-cooked
    beetroot
4 Little Gem lettuce hearts,
    broken into leaves
100g/4oz baby leaf salad leaves
handful tarragon, leaves roughly
    chopped
handful pea shoots
For the dressing
2 tsp Dijon mustard
1 tbsp cider vinegar
salt and freshly ground black
    pepper

Bring a small pan of water to the boil, carefully
spoon in the quail eggs and simmer for 2½–3
minutes. Remove using a slotted spoon and plunge
into a bowl of cold water. Keep the pan of water on
the heat and bring back to the boil. Add the peas
and simmer for 2–3 mins, until tender, then drain
and run under cold water.

Heat a drizzle of oil in a large frying pan, add the
bacon and fry until very crisp on both sides. Drain
on kitchen paper and set aside, leaving the oil in
the pan. Whisk the mustard, vinegar and some
seasoning into the bacon fat, and gently warm
through. Taste and add more mustard, vinegar or
oil as needed, set aside.

Drain the beetroot and cut into wedges, arrange
on plates with the Little Gem and baby leaves. Peel
and halve the eggs, then divide between the plates.
Snap the bacon into pieces and scatter over the
salads. Drizzle over the dressing, then sprinkle with
the tarragon and pea shoots.

AVGOLEMONO
★
LEMON & EGG SOUP

In this traditional Greek soup, the egg thickens the chicken broth, giving a silky smoothness to counter the lemon tang.

 SERVES 4

 TAKES 1 hour

1 × small (1.1kg/2¼lb) free-range
   chicken
2 bay leaves
5 peppercorns
1 red onion, quartered
250g/9oz orzo
3 eggs
5 tbsp lemon juice
handful snipped chives, to garnish
salt and freshly ground
   black pepper

Place the chicken in a large pan, cover completely with cold water and add the bay leaves, peppercorns and onion. Bring to the boil, then gently simmer for 45 minutes or until the chicken is completely cooked through. Remove the chicken and set aside until cool enough to handle. Shred the meat and discard the skin and bones. Strain the stock and transfer to a medium pan. Bring the stock to the boil over medium-high heat and simmer until reduced by half. Season to taste.

Bring a pan of salted water to the boil. Add the orzo and cook for 8 minutes. Drain and set aside.

Add the shredded chicken to the hot stock and simmer for 2 minutes.

In a bowl, whisk the eggs and lemon juice together until emulsified – it will become paler and slightly thickened. While whisking, slowly add two ladlefuls of hot stock from the pan. Gradually whisk everything back into the pan.

Over a gentle heat, cook, stirring, for about 2 minutes until the soup thickens very slightly (be careful not to let it bubble). Season to taste. Spoon the orzo between shallow bowls, ladle over the soup and garnish with chives and black pepper.

ROTHKO

RAREBIT

A Rothko-esque vision where eggs are cooked into thick
slices of bread and covered with a blanket of Welsh rarebit.
Just remember to watch the rarebit toasting under
the grill like a hawk.

 SERVES 2

 TAKES 10 minutes

2 thick (2.5cm) slices country-style
   bread
1 egg yolk plus 2 whole eggs
1 tsp English mustard
70g/2½oz finely grated mature
   Cheddar
1 tbsp beer
1 tsp Worcestershire sauce
dash of Tabasco
15g/½oz butter, melted

Preheat the grill to medium-high. Use a 5cm/2
inch round cutter (or glass) to cut out a hole in the
centre of each slice of bread. To make the rarebit
mixture, mix the egg yolk, mustard, cheese, beer,
Worcestershire sauce and Tabasco together in a
bowl. Set to one side.

Brush both sides of bread with some of the melted
butter. Place a non-stick frying pan over medium
heat, add the buttered bread and toast for 10
seconds. Pour a little splash of melted butter into
the centre of each 'hole' and crack an egg into
each. Leave for 1–2 minutes, or until the whites
look as though they are about halfway set. Then
carefully flip with a fish slice, and cook for another
minute or until the white has completely set.
Transfer to a baking sheet.

Spread the rarebit mixture onto each of the toasts
and place under the grill for 1–2 minutes – keep
your eyes on them – until golden, melted and
bubbling. Serve straight away – the yolk should still
be runny.

OEUFS

AU PLAT

Serve these 'eggs on a plate' simply dressed with the browned buttery juices from the pan and pimped up with garlicky fried mushrooms.

 SERVES 2

 TAKES 10 minutes

200g/7oz mixed wild mushrooms, such as shiitake, oyster or enoki
30g/1oz butter
1 garlic clove, crushed
few thyme sprigs
handful chopped flat-leaf parsley
4 eggs
salt and freshly ground black pepper

Brush the mushrooms clean and slice them. Melt half the butter in a pan over medium heat. Fry the garlic for 30 seconds, then add the mushrooms, thyme and season with salt and pepper. Increase the heat to high and cook for 4–5 minutes, then fold through the parsley.

Meanwhile in a separate pan, melt the remaining butter over medium heat. Break two of the eggs into a cup, being careful not to pierce the yolks, then pour into the pan. Cover the pan for 30 seconds, then uncover and cook for about 1½ minutes, until the whites have set. Season and slide the eggs onto a plate. Cook the remaining eggs in the same way. Spoon the herby mushrooms and any butter from the pan over the top and serve.

EGG MAYO
★
OPEN SANDWICH

Egg and cress must be one of the greatest sandwich fillings. Done 'properly' using home-made mayonnaise, and with the addition of salty anchovies, you'll be pushed to find a more pleasurable sandwich.

 SERVES 4

 TAKES 15 minutes

6 eggs
6 tbsp mayonnaise (see page 88 for home-made)
½ tsp English mustard
20g/¾oz (about 5) roughly chopped white anchovies (optional)
1 punnet of cress, leaves snipped
4 slices dark wholemeal (wholegrain) or rye bread, toasted
freshly ground black pepper

Place the eggs in a pan, cover with cold water, bring to the boil and cook for 6 minutes. Drain and plunge the eggs into a bowl of iced water to cool, then peel and chop.

Mix the mayonnaise and mustard together in a bowl, then fold through the chopped egg, making sure it's all well coated. Stir through the anchovies and most of the snipped cress. Pile onto the toasted bread, scatter with the remaining cress and lots of freshly ground black pepper.

EGG DROP
★
SOUP

This is a comforting bowl of remedial goodness. The eggs
are poured into the hot chicken broth, forming shaggy,
noodly strands.

  SERVES 4 as an appetiser

TAKES 25 minutes

950ml/1 quart good-quality
   chicken stock
1 tbsp soy sauce
5cm/2 inch piece root ginger,
   peeled and sliced
½ tsp Sichuan pepper
2 star anise
1 cinnamon stick
1 tbsp brown miso paste
150g/5½oz shiitake or chestnut
   mushrooms, cleaned and sliced
1½ tbsp cornflour (cornstarch)
2 eggs
4 spring onions (scallions), finely
   sliced, to serve
1 red chilli pepper, finely sliced,
   to serve

Pour the stock into a pan and add the soy sauce,
ginger and spices. Bring to the boil then simmer
over low heat, covered, for 15 minutes. Remove the
aromatics using a slotted spoon and discard. Stir
the miso paste into the broth, add the mushrooms
and simmer, uncovered, for a further 5 minutes.

In a bowl, mix 1 tablespoon cornflour (cornstarch)
with a little of the hot broth to make a paste, then
whisk back into the pan and let it simmer for 2
minutes to thicken slightly.

Whisk the remaining cornflour with the eggs in
a bowl, then slowly drizzle the mixture into the
barely simmering soup, gently whisking with a
fork or chopsticks at the same time to create tiny
strands of egg. Take off the heat and leave to stand
for 1 minute. Serve in small bowls topped with the
spring onions (scallions) and chilli pepper.

SMOKIE

★

EN COCOTTE

Arbroath smokies are a hot-smoked haddock produced in small smokehouses in Arbroath, Scotland.

 SERVES 4

 TAKES 30 minutes
plus cooling

200ml/7fl oz double (heavy) cream
1 tbsp grain mustard
juice of ½ small lemon
150g/5½oz Arbroath smokie or
  kippers
butter, to grease
1 tbsp chopped dill plus extra for
  sprinkling
4 duck eggs or large hen eggs
4 tsp crème fraîche
bunch asparagus, woody ends
  snapped off
salt and freshly ground black
  pepper

Heat the cream in a small pan over medium heat until boiling. Allow to bubble away for 3 minutes, then remove from the heat and add the mustard and lemon. Pour into a bowl and leave to cool.

Cook the smokies in the microwave or under the grill. When cool enough to handle, remove the skin and flake the flesh, discarding the skin and any large bones. Leave to cool completely.

Preheat the oven to 180°C/350°F/gas 4. Grease four 160ml/5½fl oz ramekins with butter. Fold the smokies and dill through the mustard cream, then spoon the mixture between ramekins. Break an egg into each. Season, then put a spoonful of crème fraîche on top of each egg yolk and sprinkle with a little dill.

Arrange the ramekins in a deep ovenproof dish or roasting tin. Pour just-boiled water into the dish or tin to reach halfway up the sides of the ramekins. Transfer to the oven to bake for 18–20 minutes, or until the egg whites have set.

Meanwhile, bring a pan of salted water to the boil and blanch the asparagus for 3–4 minutes until tender.

Carefully remove the baked eggs from the oven, then serve with asparagus soldiers for dipping.

EGG

FOO YUNG

A lacy golden omelette punctuated with crunchy vegetables and roast pork with a sweet and salty gravy, this is a great way to use up leftovers.

SERVES 2

TAKES 15 minutes

4 eggs
2 tbsp chicken stock
40g/1½oz beansprouts
40g/1½oz shiitake mushrooms, sliced
2 spring onions (scallions), finely sliced plus 1 to garnish
½ red (bell) pepper, deseeded and finely sliced
30g/1oz water chestnuts, drained and finely chopped
1 large garlic clove, finely chopped
40g/1½oz leftover roast pork or cooked prawns, finely chopped
1 tbsp groundnut oil
salt and freshly ground black pepper

For the sauce
200ml/7fl oz chicken stock
2 tbsp soy sauce
1½ tsp Chinese rice vinegar
1½ tsp sugar
1 tbsp cornflour (cornstarch)

First make the omelette mixture. Whisk the eggs in a bowl with some seasoning and the 2 tablespoons of chicken stock. Add the vegetables, water chestnuts, garlic and pork, and combine well with a fork or chopsticks until evenly coated.

To make the sauce, pour the 200ml/7fl oz chicken stock into a pan and add the soy sauce, rice vinegar and sugar, then bring to the boil over high heat. In a small bowl, mix the cornflour (cornstarch) with 2 tablespoons of the boiling sauce to make a paste then whisk the mixture back into the pan and simmer over low heat for 2 minutes. Remove from the heat and set aside.

Heat half the oil in a small frying pan over medium-high heat. Add half the omelette mixture, tipping the pan to evenly coat the surface. Cook for 2–3 minutes or until the base is golden and the eggs are just about set. Fold one side over the other, forming a half-moon and then wiggle it onto a warm plate. Repeat with the remaining mixture and oil. Spoon over the gravy and garnish with a little sliced spring onion (scallion).

SNACK

★

EGGS

PINK

★

PICKLED EGGS

These pretty inky-pink eggs infused with beetroot, spices and bay, taste as spectacular as they look. They are all the better when left for two or three weeks before eating, allowing the flavours to mellow.

 SERVES 6

 TAKES 20 minutes, plus cooling and pickling time

6 eggs
200ml/7fl oz red wine vinegar
150ml/5fl oz cider vinegar
1 tsp demerara sugar
1 tsp sea salt
2 tsp coriander seeds
1 tsp mustard seeds
10 allspice berries
1 large cooked beetroot, peeled and sliced
2 fresh bay leaves
2 garlic cloves, peeled
½ red onion, peeled and cut into wedges

Place the eggs in a pan, cover with cold water and bring to the boil over medium-high heat. Turn the heat right down and gently simmer for 10 minutes. Drain and plunge into cold running water to cool quickly, then carefully peel.

Pour the vinegars into a small pan along with 200ml/7fl oz water, the sugar, sea salt and the spices. Place over high heat, bring to the boil, then reduce the heat and simmer for 5 minutes. Remove from the heat and set aside for 10 minutes to let the flavours infuse.

Layer the eggs, beetroot slices, bay leaves, garlic and onion into a sterilised 1 litre/1 quart glass jar. Top with the cooled vinegar, and spices, to cover. Seal the jar then gently tip to the side to ensure the pickling liquid touches the entire surface of each egg. Refrigerate and leave for at least 3 days, and up to 3 months, before eating.

CURRIED

★

EGG MAYONNAISE

Spice up a traditional egg mayonnaise with hints of curry.
This also makes a delicious filling sandwiched between
thick slices of soft buttered farmhouse bread.

 SERVES 4

 TAKES 20 minutes

3 eggs
3 tbsp mayonnaise (see page 88
  for home-made)
1 tsp curry powder
1 tsp lemon juice
1 tsp mango chutney
½ celery stick, finely diced
1 spring onion (scallion),
  finely diced
20g/¾oz plump sultanas
1 Little Gem, leaves separated
pinch of smoked paprika, to dust
few coriander (cilantro) leaves,
  to garnish
salt and freshly ground
  black pepper

Place the eggs in a pan, cover with cold water and
bring to the boil over medium-high heat. Lower the
heat and simmer for 6 minutes. Drain and plunge
the eggs into a bowl of iced water to cool quickly.
Peel and chop.

Mix the mayo, curry powder, lemon juice and
chutney together. Season, then fold through the
chopped egg, celery, spring onion and sultanas.
Arrange eight Little Gem leaves on a plate, spoon
the curried egg between them. Dust with a pinch
of paprika and garnish with a few coriander
(cilantro) leaves.

QUAIL EGGS WITH
★
FLAVOURED SALTS

Flavoured salts can be stored in airtight jars for up to three months and used to add a pop of flavour to grilled meats, salads, roast vegetables and even popcorn.

 MAKES 3 salts

 TAKES 40 minutes

12 quail eggs
For the spiced sesame salt
1 tbsp sesame seeds
1 tsp fennel seeds
1 tsp cumin seeds
3 tbsp sea salt
For the lemon oregano salt
zest of 1 large lemon
4 tbsp sea salt
1½ tsp dried oregano
For the smoky sweet salt
1 tsp smoked sweet paprika
1 tsp cayenne
3 tbsp sea salt

Bring a large pan of water to the boil. Carefully lower in your eggs and simmer for 3 minutes. Remove with a slotted spoon and immediately rinse under cold running water to cool.

Make each salt in turn. Toast the sesame, fennel and cumin seeds in a small, dry pan for a couple of minutes until fragrant. Mix with the sea salt then blitz in a mini processor (or grind using a pestle and mortar) until you have a fine powder.

Preheat the oven to 200°C/400°F/gas 6 and line a lipped baking tray with baking parchment. Mix the lemon zest and salt together in a small bowl. Spread over the lined tray, place in the hot oven then immediately turn off the heat and leave the tray in the oven for 30 minutes. Remove and stir through the oregano. If you prefer a finer texture, you can grind it as per the spiced sesame salt.

Mix the paprika and cayenne in a mortar and pestle (or mini processor), then add the salt and grind together.

Serve the three salts in separate little bowls with the quail eggs for peeling and dipping.

EGG-FRIED

★

RICE CAKES

These mini egg-fried rice cakes are perfect for a snack, but the rice can also be a meal in its own right, especially if you throw in a few extra ingredients. This is fantastic for using up any leftovers and you can opt simply to make the rice rather than shaping into cakes.

 MAKES 12

 TAKES 30 minutes, plus soaking, cooling and chilling

100g/3½oz risotto rice
1 tbsp sesame oil
4 spring onions (scallions), finely sliced
1 fat garlic clove, finely chopped
¼ tsp chilli flakes (red pepper flakes)
80g/3oz frozen shelled edamame, defrosted
3 eggs, beaten
1 tbsp soy sauce
handful coriander (cilantro) leaves, finely chopped
4 tbsp panko breadcrumbs
groundnut oil, for shallow-frying
sweet chilli sauce, to serve

Place the rice in a pan with 200ml/7fl oz salted water. Bring to the boil, then cover and simmer gently for 10 minutes. Remove from the heat and leave, covered, for 10 minutes, or until the water is absorbed and the rice tender.

Heat the sesame oil in a large frying pan. Add the spring onions (scallions), garlic and chilli flakes. Stir-fry over high heat for 1 minute. Add the edamame and rice, and pour in the whisked eggs. When the bottom starts to set, use a wooden spoon to scramble the eggs. Remove from the heat, add the soy sauce and fork through the rice. Spread the rice over a large plate, press cling film (plastic wrap) onto the surface, and leave to cool for 10 minutes.

Transfer the rice to a bowl and mix through the coriander (cilantro). Using wet hands, divide the rice into 12 small cakes. Press the top and bottom lightly into some breadcrumbs, then chill for 15 minutes. Heat enough oil in a large frying pan to come up to about 1cm/½ inch up the sides. Fry the cakes in batches for 2–3 minutes each side, until golden, crisp and piping hot throughout. Serve with sweet chilli sauce for dipping.

BABY BAKED

★

EGGS IN POTATOES

These are best eaten warm, so prepare them in advance
and, when ready to serve, crack in your quail eggs and
pop them in the oven. Choose medium-sized potatoes
to allow room for the egg.

 MAKES 24 canapés

 TAKES 1 hour, plus cooling

12 medium-sized Charlotte
potatoes (or other waxy
new potato)
½ tbsp olive oil
30g/1oz finely grated Cheddar
2 tbsp soured cream, plus extra
to serve
handful snipped chives
2 spring onions (scallions),
trimmed and finely chopped
24 quail eggs
salt and freshly ground
black pepper

Preheat the oven to 220°C/430°F/gas 8. Place the
potatoes on a baking tray, drizzle with oil and
season with salt and pepper, and roll around to
cover. Roast for 45 minutes until crisp and golden.
Remove and set aside until cool enough to handle.
Cut each potato in half lengthways and with a
small teaspoon, scoop out the flesh into a bowl,
leaving a good amount around the edges to
support the skins.

Mash the potato flesh a little with a fork to get rid
of any large lumps then fold through the grated
cheese, soured cream, chives and spring onions
(scallions). Season with salt and pepper.

Scoop the potato mixture back into the skins, make
a depression in the middle of each one (in which
you'll bake the eggs) and place on a baking tray.
Crack each egg in turn, letting a little of the white
drain into a bowl, before filling the potato skins.
Season with a little salt and pepper.

Bake in the oven for 8 minutes, or until the egg
whites have set. Remove and serve while warm with
soured cream for dipping.

HOME-MADE
★
MAYONNAISE

With a little patience, home-made mayonnaise is surprisingly simple to whip together and bears no resemblance to the long-life, vinegary shop-bought variety. Once you've mastered it, use it a base for tartare sauce, aioli or remoulade.

 MAKES 280g

 TAKES 5 minutes

2 egg yolks
1 tsp English mustard powder
2 tsp white wine vinegar
½ tsp salt plus extra to taste
squeeze of lemon juice or to taste
80ml/2½fl oz olive oil
200ml/7fl oz groundnut oil
crudités such as radishes, celery
  sticks or steamed asparagus
  spears, to serve
freshly ground black pepper

Whisk the egg yolks with the mustard, vinegar, salt and a few good grinds of pepper in a bowl. Squeeze over a little lemon juice and whisk in.

Very slowly, add the oils a drop at a time, whisking really well between each addition. Once an emulsion begins to form you can begin to add the oil in a thin trickle, whisking all the time, until you have a lovely creamy mayo. Check the seasoning and add more salt, pepper or lemon juice if needed.

Serve with crudités of your choice. Spicy radishes, sticks of celery and steamed asparagus spears are all good.

BLACK PUDDING
★
SCOTCH EGGS

Here black pudding and egg are teamed up to make the
most perfect match. Eat them warm with spicy mustard.

 MAKES 6

 TAKES 1 hour

8 eggs, at room temperature
350g/12½oz pork mince
200g/7oz black pudding, crumbled
4 tbsp chopped flat-leaf parsley,
   sage and thyme leaves
1 plump garlic clove, finely
   chopped
55g/2oz plain (all-purpose) flour,
   seasoned with salt and pepper
80g/3oz panko or fresh
   breadcrumbs
vegetable oil, for deep-frying
English mustard, to serve
sea salt and freshly ground black
   pepper

Bring a medium pan of water to the boil. Carefully
lower in six of the eggs and simmer for 6 minutes.
Remove with a slotted spoon, plunge into a bowl of
iced water to cool quickly, then carefully peel.

In a bowl, with your hands, mix the mince, black
pudding, parsley and garlic. Season well with a
pinch of salt and plenty of pepper then divide into
six portions (each about 95g/3½oz). Flatten each
portion into a 13cm/5 inch circle. Working with one
portion and one egg at a time, place the egg in the
centre of the black pudding mixture. Use your hands
to mould the mixture up and around to encase the
egg completely. Place on a plate lined with kitchen
paper and chill for 20 minutes.

In a shallow bowl, lightly beat the remaining two
eggs. Put the seasoned flour and breadcrumbs in
two separate shallow bowls. Dust each encased
egg first in the flour, then in the egg and finally
the breadcrumbs. Set aside.

Heat the oil in a large, deep-sided pan to 180°C/
350°F/gas 4 on a thermometer (or drop in a cube of
bread – it will turn golden in 60 seconds when the oil
is ready). Deep-fry two eggs at a time for 8 minutes,
until crisp and golden. Remove with a slotted spoon
and drain on kitchen paper. Sprinkle with sea salt and
serve warm or cold with English mustard.

JAPANESE

★

OMELETTE SUSHI

Traditionally this omelette is cooked in a rectangular
tamago pan – the straight sides make rolling easy and even.

 MAKES 8 pieces

 TAKES 45 minutes,
plus cooling

140g/5oz sushi rice, rinsed well
  and drained
1½ tbsp rice wine vinegar
3 tsp sugar
1 tsp salt
1 sheet nori, cut into
  1cm/½ inch strips
1 tbsp caviar (optional), to garnish
micro leaves, such as red
  amaranth, to garnish

For the omelette
4 eggs
4 tbsp dashi or vegetable stock
1 tbsp mirin
1 tsp soy sauce plus extra to serve
a little groundnut oil, to grease

Put the rice into a pan with 300ml/10fl oz cold water.
Bring to the boil, then simmer gently for 10 minutes.
Remove from the heat, cover and leave to stand for
10 minutes. Mix the rice vinegar, 2 teaspoons of the
sugar and the salt in a small bowl until the sugar has
dissolved. Fork the vinegar mixture through the rice,
and set aside.

In a bowl, whisk the eggs with the dashi, mirin and
soy sauce. Grease a frying pan well with oil and place
over medium-high heat. Add a quarter of the egg
mixture, tilting the pan to coat the surface, and cook
for 1–2 minutes until almost set. Using a fish slice,
flip and fold the omelette up, about 4cm at a time,
to make a roll. Leave to one side of the pan. Grease
the pan with a little more oil then pour a third of the
remaining egg mixture into the pan, coating the base
and making sure it runs under the folded omelette.
Cook for 1–2 minutes, then fold, and repeat the
process until you have used up all the egg mixture.
Transfer the omelette to a chopping board and place
a heavy tray on top (this will help to squeeze out
the excess liquid). Leave to cool before cutting into
2.5cm/1 inch thick slices.

With wet fingers, shape the rice into neat rectangles
(2cm/¾ inch deep and 2.5cm/1 inch wide). Top each
with a slice of egg, wrap with a strip of nori, then
garnish with caviar, if using, and a few micro leaves.
Serve with soy sauce for dipping.

DEVILLED

★

EGGS

A retro canapé but wickedly delicious. Bring back
devilled eggs to your drinks party and you're guaranteed
to impress your guests.

 MAKES 12

 TAKES 20 minutes

6 eggs
3 tbsp mayonnaise (see page 88
    for home-made)
1 tsp white wine vinegar
1 tsp English mustard
dash of Sriracha hot sauce
¼ tsp celery salt
1 tbsp snipped chives
smoked paprika, to sprinkle

Place the eggs in a pan, cover with cold water and
bring to the boil over high heat. Lower the heat
right down to a shudder and gently simmer for 10
minutes. Drain and cool under cold running water
then peel and slice each egg in half.

Scoop the yolks into a bowl, mash with a fork
and set the egg whites aside. Stir the mayonnaise,
vinegar, mustard, hot sauce, celery salt and most of
the chives through the egg yolks, then spoon into
a small piping bag fitted with a star nozzle. Pipe the
mixture into the egg white halves and sprinkle with
pinch of paprika and a few chives to serve.

GRIBICHE

★

DIP

Gribiche is a classic French sauce with similar flavourings to tartare. Its mayonnaise base is made by beating the cooked yolks until emulsified, and the whites are chopped and folded through.

 SERVES 4

 TAKES 20 minutes

2 large eggs
1 tsp Dijon mustard
2 tsp white vinegar
100ml/3½fl oz light oil
½ tsp Worcestershire sauce
1½ tbsp finely diced cornichons
1½ tbsp chopped capers
2 tbsp chopped herbs, such as
   tarragon, dill and chives
toasted sourdough or steamed
   asparagus spears, to serve
salt and freshly ground
   black pepper

Bring a small pan of water to the boil and carefully lower in the eggs. Simmer for 10 minutes. Drain and cool under cold running water, then peel and slice each egg in half. Scoop the yolks into a bowl, mash with a fork, then pass through a sieve into a bowl. Roughly chop the egg whites.

Add the mustard, vinegar, salt and pepper to the bowl with the egg yolks and whisk together. Very slowly, a drop at a time at first, pour in the oil, whisking as you do so to form an emulsion. When all the oil has been added, season with salt and pepper to taste, then stir through the remaining ingredients and the chopped egg whites. Serve with toasted sourdough or steamed asparagus.

CHINESE

★

MARBLED TEA EGGS

These beautiful eggs, steeped in a tea-infused liquid, are celebrated as a symbol of prosperity at Chinese New Year. Don't be shy when you crack the shell; the deeper the cracks, the stronger the marbling.

 MAKES 8

 TAKES 1 hour 10 minutes, plus cooling and steeping time

8 eggs
120ml/4fl oz soy sauce
3 tbsp light brown soft sugar
½ tsp Sichuan pepper
½ tsp fennel seeds
8 cloves
2 star anise
1 cinnamon stick
3 pieces orange peel
1 tbsp loose-leaf lapsang souchong tea

Place the eggs in a pan, cover with cold water and bring to the boil over medium-high heat. Lower the heat and simmer for 3 minutes. Remove with a slotted spoon, and plunge the eggs into a bowl of iced water to cool quickly. Using the back of a teaspoon, crack the shells all over.

Pour the water from the pan, return the eggs and add the soy sauce, sugar, dried spices, orange peel and enough water to cover. Bring to the boil over high heat, add the tea leaves, then turn the heat right down, cover and gently simmer for 1 hour. Remove from the heat and leave to cool in the pan.

Transfer the eggs in their liquid to the fridge to steep for at least 24 hours, 3 days is best. The longer you leave them, the stronger the flavour and the more defined the marbling. Remove and peel to eat. They will keep, unpeeled, in the fridge for up to 3 days.

SAUSAGE & EGG

★

PICNIC ROLLS

With baby eggs nestling inside, these mustard sausage rolls
are the perfect portable snack or ideal for eating greedily
straight from the oven.

MAKES 6

TAKES 45 minutes,
plus chilling

400g/14oz sausage meat
1 tsp English mustard
2 tsp wholegrain mustard
1 tbsp chopped tarragon leaves
1½ tbsp chopped flat-leaf
    parsley leaves
12 quail eggs
320g/11½oz ready-rolled all-butter
    puff pastry
1 egg yolk, beaten
2 tbsp poppy seeds, to sprinkle

Mix the sausage meat together with the mustards,
tarragon and parsley in a bowl. Bring a pan of
water to the boil, lower in the eggs and cook for
2 minutes. Drain and transfer the eggs to a bowl
of iced water to cool quickly, then carefully peel.

Unroll the pastry and cut into six 8cm x 13.5cm
(3 x 5½ inch) rectangles. Take a sixth of the sausage
meat, shape it into an 8cm x 11cm (3 x 4½ inch)
rectangle and lay two eggs along the middle, nose
to tail. Wrap the sausage meat around to form a
neat roll with the eggs in the centre, and place on
top of a piece of pastry. Brush with a little beaten
egg yolk and roll the pastry to encase and seal
underneath. Repeat with the remaining pastry and
sausage meat, then chill for 20 minutes. Preheat the
oven to 200°/400°F/gas 6 and line a baking sheet
with baking parchment.

Place the sausage rolls on the lined baking sheet.
Brush all over with egg and sprinkle with poppy
seeds. Bake in the oven for 25 minutes, until crisp,
golden and cooked through. Serve warm or cold.

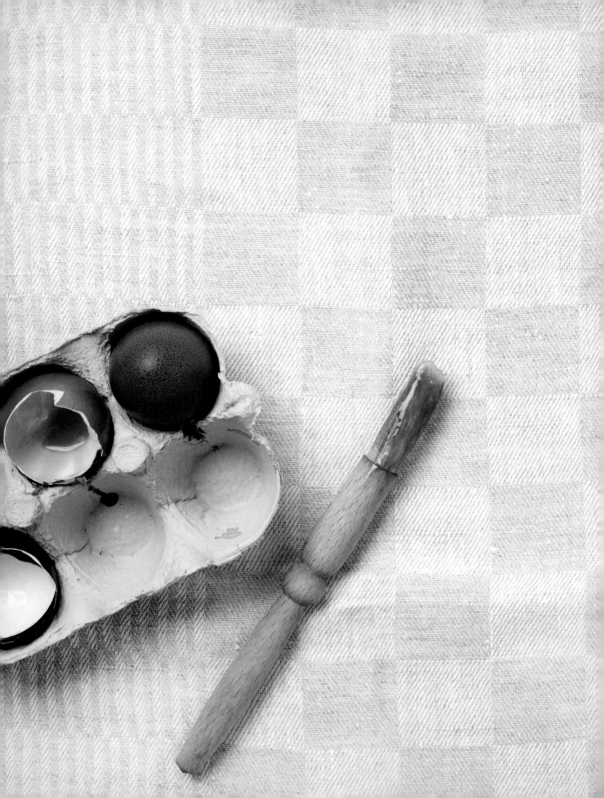

SUPPER

★

EGGS

FLORENTINE
★
PIZZA

Home-made pizza wins hands down when compared to a lukewarm soggy-bottomed takeaway one. You can freeze the dough after the first rise, then simply defrost, roll out and top whenever you fancy.

 SERVES 4

 TAKES 40 minutes, plus rising

For the pizza base
1 × 7g/¼oz sachet fast-action dried yeast
1 tsp sugar
225g/½lb strong white bread flour
1 tsp salt
olive oil, to grease
semolina, to dust

First make the pizza base. Pour 100ml/3½fl oz lukewarm water into a bowl. Sprinkle the yeast and sugar over the surface, whisk with a fork then set aside for 5 minutes in a warm place until frothy.

Sift the flour and salt into a large bowl. Make a well in the centre. Pour in the yeast mixture along with 50ml/2fl oz lukewarm water, and mix quickly to form a soft, pliable dough. Knead on a lightly floured surface for 8–10 minutes, until smooth. Shape into a ball then place in a lightly oiled bowl and cover with cling film (plastic wrap). Set aside to rise for 1 hour, or until doubled in size. Punch down on the dough to remove any large air bubbles. Divide into two and roll each portion into a ball. Cover loosely with oiled cling film and set aside for 20 minutes.

Preheat the oven to 220°C/430°F/gas 8 and put two baking sheets inside to heat up.

ingredients and method continue overleaf...

★ ★ ★ ★ ★ ★ ★ ★ ★ ★ ★ ★ ★ ★ ★ ★

★ ★

FLORENTINE PIZZA
continued...

For the pizza topping
160g/6oz tomato passata,
    seasoned with dried oregano,
    salt and pepper
125g/4½oz mozzarella, torn
150g/5½oz baby spinach, wilted
    and well-drained
1 small red chilli pepper, finely
    sliced
55g/2oz spicy Italian salami
4 eggs
20g/3/4oz finely grated Parmesan
extra virgin olive oil, to drizzle
a handful of basil leaves
salt and freshly ground
    black pepper

Stretch and roll each ball of dough into a 28cm/11 inch disc. Sprinkle the hot baking sheets with semolina and put one base on each. Spread the tomato passata thinly over the bases leaving a border around the edge. Scatter with the mozzarella, spinach, chilli pepper and salami, Make two 'nests' in the topping of each pizza and crack an egg into each. Finally, sprinkle over the Parmesan and season with salt and pepper. Cook in the oven for 10–12 minutes. Drizzle with extra virgin olive oil, tear over the basil leaves and serve.

SALMON QUICHE
★
WITH PINK PEPPERCORNS

This quiche oozes sophistication, is seriously pretty and has a wonderful intense flavour. The kind of food that is perfect for late summer al fresco eating.

 SERVES 6

 TAKES 1 hour, plus chilling

For the pastry
200g/7oz plain (all-purpose) flour plus extra for dusting
½ tsp salt
100g/3½oz cold butter, cut into cubes plus a knob to fry
1 egg yolk

First, make the pastry. Whizz the flour with the salt in a food processor. Add the butter and pulse until like fine breadcrumbs. Add the egg yolk and 2 tbsp iced water. Pulse until the mixture starts to clump together. Bring together into a flat disc with your hands, wrap in cling film (plastic wrap) and chill for 20 minutes.

Roll the pastry out on a lightly floured surface and use it to line a 20cm/8 inch loose-bottomed tart tin, trimming off the excess. Prick the base with a fork and chill in the freezer for 20 minutes.

Preheat the oven to 200°C/400°F/gas 6 with a baking sheet inside. Line the pastry with baking parchment and fill with ceramic beans, and place on the hot baking sheet. Bake for 12 minutes then remove the paper and beans and put back in the oven for another 5 minutes. Remove and set aside to cool. Reduce the temperature to 180°C/350°C/gas 4.

ingredients and method continue overleaf...

★ ★ ★ ★ ★ ★ ★ ★ ★ ★ ★ ★ ★ ★ ★ ★

★ ★

SALMON QUICHE

continued...

For the filling
knob of butter
1 small onion, finely sliced
170g/6oz hot-smoked salmon,
    skinless and flaked
130g/4½oz burrata, drained and
    torn into pieces
30g/1oz watercress leaves,
    chopped
2 tbsp chopped soft herbs, such as
    dill, tarragon or chervil
2 large eggs
200ml/7fl oz double (heavy) cream
½ tsp pink peppercorns,
    lightly crushed
salt, to season

Next, melt a knob of butter in a frying pan and add the onion. Cook over low heat for 5 minutes, until softened. Remove from the heat and set aside to cool. Spoon the onions inside the pastry case and top with the salmon, burrata and most of the watercress and herbs. Whisk the eggs and cream together and season with salt, then pour into the pastry case. Scatter with the remaining watercress, herbs and pink peppercorns. Place on the baking sheet in the oven and bake for 30 minutes, or until the filling has set and the surface is golden. Serve warm.

MUSSELS WITH

★

SAFFRON CUSTARD

Saffron is a beautiful ingredient. Here, it turns a simple bowl of mussels into a golden gem of a dish. Serve with plenty of buttered crusty bread for mopping up the juices.

 SERVES 2

 TAKES 15 minutes

good pinch of saffron threads
1 tbsp rapeseed oil
2 banana shallots, finely chopped
1 fat garlic clove, finely chopped
200ml/7fl oz dry white wine
900g/2lb fresh mussels, cleaned
   and debearded (discard any
   with broken shells or that
   remain open when tapped)
1 large egg yolk
1 tsp plain (all-purpose) flour
1 tsp curry powder
200ml/7fl oz double (heavy) cream
   or crème fraîche
handful flat-leaf parsley leaves,
   chopped

Put the saffron in a small bowl, pour over 1 tablespoon just-boiled water and leave to soak.

Heat the oil in a large pan. Add the shallots and cook over medium heat for 3 minutes, until softened. Stir through the garlic and continue to cook for a minute or so. Pour over the wine, let it sizzle, then tumble in the mussels. Cover with a lid and leave to cook for 3–4 minutes, shaking the pan occasionally.

Remove the mussels with a slotted spoon into a bowl, discarding any that haven't opened. Bring the cooking liquor to the boil and simmer for 3–4 minutes to reduce it by about a half. In a bowl, whisk the egg yolk with the flour and curry powder, followed by the cream and soaked saffron, along with its water. Stir the mixture into the cooking liquor, bring to a simmer then return the mussels to the pan to warm through. Sprinkle over the parsley and serve.

SALMON OMELETTE
★
SOUFFLÉ

This is really about turning an airy soufflé into something more substantial: a light salmon, herb and cheese omelette.

 SERVES 4

 TAKES 25 minutes,
plus cooling

30g/1oz butter, plus a knob
for frying
1½ tbsp plain (all-purpose) flour
150ml/5fl oz full-fat (whole) milk
100ml/3½fl oz double (heavy)
cream
55g/2oz grated Parmesan
55g/2oz fine asparagus, woody
ends snapped off
5 eggs, separated
140g/5oz smoked salmon, chopped
handful finely chopped herbs,
such as dill, chives, parsley
grated zest of 1 lemon
80g/3oz cream cheese
salt and freshly ground
black pepper

Melt the butter in a pan over medium heat, add the flour and cook for 1 minute, stirring with a wooden spoon. Gradually pour in the milk and cream, stirring as you do so, to make a smooth sauce. Let it bubble for a minute or so until thickened. Add the Parmesan and season with pepper, then spoon into bowl and set aside to cool.

Bring a pan of salted water to the boil and cook the asparagus for 2–3 minutes, until tender. Drain well and cut into 2.5cm/1 inch lengths.

Stir the egg yolks, salmon, asparagus, herbs and lemon zest through the cooled cheese sauce. Then add spoonfuls of the cream cheese. In a separate bowl, whisk the egg whites with a pinch of salt to form stiff peaks. Add a spoonful to the salmon mixture to loosen, then fold the rest through, keeping as much air in the mixture as possible.

Preheat the grill to medium-high. Melt a knob of butter in a 23cm/9 inch ovenproof pan, add the mixture and cook over medium heat for 4–5 minutes. Transfer to the grill and brown the surface of the soufflé for 5–6 minutes, or until golden, risen and cooked (it should be a little gooey in the centre). Serve straight from the pan.

EGG-WHITE OMELETTE
★
BÉARNAISE AND CHIPS

A twist on a 'healthy' egg-white omelette, this dish puts the
egg yolks to use in a rich buttery Béarnaise sauce.

 SERVES 2

 TAKES 35 minutes

400g/14oz Desiree potatoes,
    scrubbed and cut into chips
1 tbsp rapeseed oil
3 tbsp white vinegar
6 peppercorns
1 shallot, sliced
6 eggs, separated
110g/4oz butter, plus a knob
    for frying
2 tsp chopped tarragon leaves
2 tsp chopped chervil leaves,
    or parsley
2 tsp snipped chives
3 tbsp finely grated Parmesan
salt and freshly ground
    black pepper

Preheat the oven to 200°C/400°F/gas 6. Place the
potato chips in a shallow roasting tray, toss in the
oil and season with salt and pepper. Roast for 35
minutes until golden and cooked through.

Meanwhile, make the Béarnaise. Put the vinegar,
peppercorns and shallot slices in a small pan over
high heat. Let it bubble and reduce to 1 tbsp. Strain
and set aside to cool. Melt the 110g/4oz butter in
a small pan over medium-low heat, until the white
solids appear on the surface. Remove from the heat
and set aside to cool slightly.

In the small bowl of a food processor (or by hand
using a whisk) mix two of the egg yolks with a pinch
of salt and the reduced vinegar. With the motor
running, trickle the warm melted butter in through
the funnel, drop by drop, leaving the white solids
behind. You should have a thick sauce. Stir through
half the chopped tarragon and chervil.

Whisk the egg whites with the remaining herbs,
Parmesan and seasoning. Melt a knob of butter in a
frying pan over medium heat. Pour the whites over
the base, leave for 5 seconds then begin drawing
in the sides using a wooden spoon. When almost
cooked, flip one side over the other and wiggle
onto a warm plate. Serve with the golden chips
and the warm Béarnaise sauce spooned over.

GALETTE

★

QUICHE LORRAINE

Quiche Lorraine should be light, flavoursome and tremble delightfully on your fork. Here I've encased the filling in buttery puff, ensuring it's a speedy tart to throw together.

 SERVES 6

 TAKES 45 minutes

1 tbsp olive oil
200g/7oz smoked streaky bacon, chopped
1 large onion, finely chopped
125ml double (heavy) cream
130g/4½oz crème fraîche
3 eggs, plus 1 egg yolk for brushing
85g/3oz finely grated Gruyère
230g/8oz all-butter puff pastry
plain (all-purpose) flour, to dust
salt and freshly ground black pepper

Preheat the oven to 200°C/400°F/gas 6 and put a baking sheet inside. Heat the oil in a frying pan and fry the bacon over medium heat until crisp. Remove with a slotted spoon and set aside. Add the onion to the pan and cook for 5–10 minutes, until softened, then set aside with the bacon to cool. Mix the cream, crème fraîche, eggs and Gruyère together. Season with black pepper.

Roll the pastry out on a lightly floured surface to a 29cm/11½ inch round. Use the pastry to line a 20cm/8 inch metal flan or tart tin, allowing the pastry to drape over the sides.

Spoon the onion and most of the bacon over the tart base. Pour the eggy cream over the top and sprinkle the surface with the remaining bacon. Now brush the outside of the overhanging pastry with egg yolk and carefully fold the edges over the filling. Be careful not to soak the pastry too much with the yolk as this will prevent it from rising.

Transfer to the hot baking sheet and bake for 25 minutes, until golden and just set in the centre. Remove and leave in the tin for a good 10 minutes before slicing and serving.

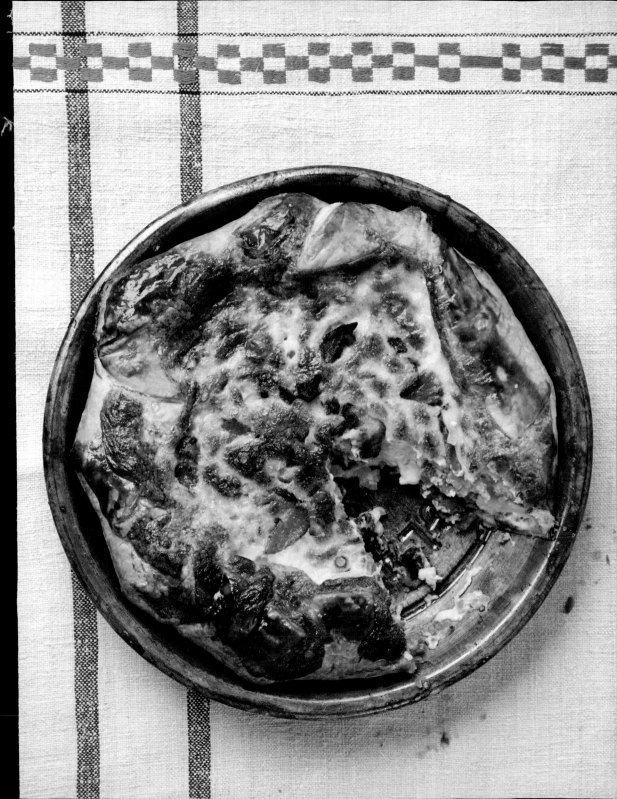

SPAGHETTI

★

CARBONARA

Eggs stirred through hot spaghetti will cook just enough
to make a rich creamy sauce, coating the pasta and
ensuring a delicious pool at the bottom of the pan.
Use good-quality smoked pancetta or bacon.

 SERVES 2

TAKES 15 minutes

200g/7oz spaghetti
2 whole eggs and 1 egg yolk
40g/1½oz finely grated Parmesan
    plus extra to serve
1 tbsp olive oil
140g/5oz cubed smoked pancetta
30g/1oz fresh breadcrumbs
handful flat-leaf parsley leaves,
    finely chopped
salt and freshly ground
    black pepper

Bring a large pan of salted water to the boil.
Add the pasta and cook for 9 minutes, or until *al
dente*. Meanwhile, mix the eggs, egg yolk and
grated Parmesan in a small bowl with a little salt
and pepper.

Heat the oil in a frying pan and fry the pancetta
over low heat until crisp. Remove with a slotted
spoon and set aside. Add the breadcrumbs to
the pan and fry for 2–3 minutes, until golden. Stir
through the parsley and set aside.

Drain the pasta, and return it to the hot pan. Pour
the eggy Parmesan mixture over the top of the
pasta and quickly mix through. Fold through the
crisped pancetta and serve sprinkled with the
parsley breadcrumbs, lots of freshly grated black
pepper and extra Parmesan.

CAESAR

★

SALAD

This is a sophisticated twist on the original. Gentleman's Relish is a powerful spread of anchovies, butter, herbs and spices. Spread sparingly.

 SERVES 2

 TAKES 20 minutes

2 eggs
6 thin slices pancetta
4 small slices sourdough or
    country-style bread
light olive oil, to drizzle
1 tbsp anchovy paste, such as
    Gentleman's Relish
few small thyme leaves
1 Romaine lettuce, outer
    leaves discarded and halved
    lengthways
shavings of Parmesan, to garnish
salt and freshly ground
    black pepper
For the dressing
1 egg yolk
1 tsp Dijon mustard
½ garlic clove, crushed
1½ tbsp lemon juice
80ml/2½fl oz light olive oil
1 tbsp natural yoghurt
3 tbsp finely grated Parmesan

To make the dressing, whisk the egg yolk with the mustard, crushed garlic, lemon juice and season with salt and pepper. Start off very slowly whisking in the oil to form an emulsion then, whisking all the time, drizzle in the remaining oil. Finally, mix in the yoghurt and Parmesan.

Bring a pan of water to the boil, gently lower in the eggs and boil for 6 minutes. Remove the eggs and rinse under cold running water to cool. Peel and cut each egg in half.

Preheat the grill to medium and line a baking tray with baking parchment. Arrange the pancetta and sourdough on the tray, drizzle with oil and grill for 1–2 minutes on each side until the toast is golden and the pancetta crisped. Remove the pancetta. Spread the toasts with anchovy paste and sprinkle with thyme leaves, then pop back under the grill for 30 seconds.

Place a wedge of lettuce on each plate and drizzle some of the dressing over the top. Add a halved egg, anchovy toasts, crisped pancetta, a good grinding of black pepper and some Parmesan shavings.

RED PEPPER
★
BAKED EGGS

Colourful, savoury and comforting, this dish has started popping up on menus everywhere because it's so easy yet so incredibly delicious.

 SERVES 4

 TAKES 40 minutes

1 tbsp olive oil
225g/8oz chorizo, thickly sliced
  on a angle
1 large onion, thickly sliced
1 tsp fennel seeds
3 red (bell) peppers, halved,
  deseeded and thickly sliced
2 garlic cloves, crushed
2 x 400g/14oz tins chopped
  tomatoes
1 tbsp tomato purée
1 tbsp sherry vinegar
4 eggs
handful parsley leaves
bread and Greek yoghurt to serve

Heat the oil over a medium heat in a large frying pan, add the chorizo and cook, stirring every so often, until the chorizo has released its lovely red oil, is cooked through and starting to crisp in places – about 5 minutes. Remove using a slotted spoon and set aside, leaving the oil in the pan.

Throw in the sliced onions, and fennel seeds and cook for 8 mins or so, until the onion has softened, adding the peppers after 2 or 3 minutes. Stir through the garlic and cook for another 1 minute. Tip in the tomatoes, and purée. Season, stir and bring to a simmer. Cook gently for 10 minutes, until thickened. Stir in the vinegar, taste and add a little sugar if needed. Using a spoon make four indents in the tomato sauce to hold the eggs, then crack them into the pan. Cover and simmer over a very low heat for 8–10 minutes, until the whites are set.

When the eggs are cooked, remove the lid and leave to cool a little. Scatter over the parsley and serve with lots of bread and dollops of Greek yoghurt.

SOLE

MALTAISE

Maltaise is a traditional hollandaise sauce blended with
blood orange juice. The buttery citrus flavours work
beautifully with seafood.

 SERVES 2

 TAKES 25 minutes

100g/3½oz fine asparagus spears
splash of olive oil
knob of butter
2 lemon soles, top skin and
  heads removed
25g/¾oz breadcrumbs
small handful chopped
  parsley leaves
salt and freshly ground
  black pepper
For the maltaise sauce
110g/4oz clarified butter plus a
  knob for frying
1 tbsp lemon juice
2 egg yolks
1 tbsp blood orange juice

To make the maltaise sauce, melt the butter in a
small pan over low heat. Set aside.

Whizz the lemon juice, egg yolks and salt and
pepper in a mini food processor, or whisk by
hand. With the motor running, very slowly pour in
the melted butter, drop by drop, until the sauce
emulsifies. Add the blood orange juice and check
the seasoning.

Meanwhile, bring a pan of salted water to the boil
and cook the asparagus for 2–3 minutes, until just
tender. Drain and set aside.

Preheat the grill to medium-high. Heat the oil and
a knob of butter in a frying pan over medium-high
heat. Season the sole, then add to the pan, skin-
side down, and fry for 2–3 minutes. Transfer the
sole to a shallow baking dish, drizzle over some of
the melted butter from the pan then pop under
the grill for 3 minutes.

Remove the sole from the heat, add the asparagus
and spoon over the maltaise sauce. Sprinkle with
breadcrumbs and parsley, and return to the grill for
4 minutes or until bubbling and golden.

EGG

CURRY

Fried and blistered boiled eggs make a rich and rewarding addition to a curry. Once cut, the warm silky yolk will flood through the spiced sauce.

 SERVES 4

 TAKES 30 minutes

3 garlic cloves, roughly chopped
5cm/2 inch piece root ginger, peeled and roughly chopped
1 red onion, roughly chopped
1 green chilli pepper, deseeded and roughly chopped
2½ tbsp ghee or groundnut oil
½ tsp yellow mustard seeds
1 tsp garam masala
½ tsp turmeric
¼ tsp smoked paprika
400g/14oz tin chopped tomatoes
3 tbsp coconut cream
120g/4oz baby spinach leaves
6 eggs
a handful chopped coriander (cilantro) leaves, to garnish
warmed chapatis, to serve
salt and freshly ground black pepper

Whizz the garlic, ginger, red onion and chilli pepper in a food processor until finely chopped (or do this by hand). Heat 1½ tablespoons of the ghee in a pan. Add the garlic and ginger paste and fry for 2 minutes over medium-high heat. Stir through all the spices and continue to fry for a further 2 minutes. Pour over the tomatoes, coconut cream and 400ml/14fl oz water. Season well with salt and pepper and simmer for 15 minutes, stirring occasionally, then add the spinach, folding through until wilted.

Meanwhile, bring a small pan of water to the boil. Carefully lower in the eggs and boil for 6 minutes. Drain and rinse under cold running water to cool quickly and then peel.

In a separate pan, heat the remaining 1 tablespoon of ghee. Add the eggs and fry over medium heat for 2–3 minutes, until blistered and golden all over. Tumble the eggs into the curry and cook for a further 1 minute. Garnish with the coriander (cilantro) leaves and serve with warmed chapatis.

BEEF

RAMEN

Make the soy-marinated eggs a day in advance. They are delicious eaten on their own or sliced through a salad.

 SERVES 2

 TAKES 30 minutes, plus marinating

For the soy-marinated eggs
2 eggs
50ml/3½ tbsp soy sauce
2 tbsp mirin
For the ramen
1 litre/1 quart good-quality beef stock
4 slices peeled root ginger
2 garlic cloves, peeled and sliced
1 red chilli pepper, deseeded and finely sliced
85g/3oz udon or ramen noodles
180g/6½oz beef sirloin or rump steak
1½ tbsp teriyaki sauce
1 tsp sesame oil, plus extra for drizzling
1 tbsp miso paste
1 tbsp soy sauce
90g/3oz baby pak choi, leaves separated
55g/2oz beansprouts
To garnish
2 spring onions (scallions), finely shredded
1 lime, cut into wedges

Cook the eggs a day in advance. Bring a small pan of water to the boil, carefully lower in the eggs and boil for 6 minutes. Rinse under cold running water to cool quickly then peel. Place the eggs in a small resealable plastic bag with the soy sauce and mirin. Refrigerate for 4 hours, or overnight, to marinate.

The next day, drain the eggs and set aside to come up to room temperature.

Pour the stock into a pan, add the ginger, garlic and most of the chilli. Bring to the boil then gently simmer over medium-low heat for 15 minutes.

Meanwhile, bring a large pan of water to the boil and cook the noodles for 6–8 minutes, or until soft. Drain and set aside while you cook the beef.

Heat a frying pan over high heat. Brush the beef with half the teriyaki sauce and sesame oil. Add to the pan and sear for 1–2 minutes each side. Remove from the heat, brush with the remaining teriyaki sauce and slice on an angle – it should be rare.

Stir the miso and soy sauce into the broth. Add the beef, pak choi and beansprouts and stir to warm through. Spoon the noodles into serving bowls and ladle over the soup. Halve the eggs and arrange on top. Drizzle with sesame oil and garnish with the spring onions, reserved chilli and lime wedges.

COBB

★

SALAD

A chopped salad, the components are remembered by the mnemonic EAT COBB: egg, avocado, tomato, chicken, onion, bacon, blue cheese, and then add lettuce.

 SERVES 4

 TAKES 35 minutes

2 large chicken breasts
1 tbsp olive oil
1 tsp ras el hanout
200g/7oz smoked streaky bacon, chopped
4 eggs
180g/6½oz cherry tomatoes
2 ripe avocados, peeled and stoned
5 spring onions (scallions)
1 large Romaine lettuce, outer leaves discarded
punnet of cress, snipped

For the dressing

55g/2oz soft blue cheese, such as Dolcelatte
2 tbsp soured cream
½ tsp Dijon mustard
2 tbsp extra virgin olive oil
1 tbsp lemon juice
small handful dill leaves

Preheat the oven to 200°C/400°F/gas 6.

Drizzle the oil over the chicken breasts and rub in the ras el hanout and seasoning. Place in a shallow roasting tray and cook in the oven for 15 minutes. Add the bacon to the tin and continue to roast for 10 minutes, or until the chicken is cooked through and the bacon crisp.

Meanwhile, bring a small pan of water to the boil. Carefully lower in your eggs and boil for 7 minutes. Remove and rinse briefly under cold running water to cool, then peel.

Next, whisk the dressing ingredients together in a food processor or by hand.

Chop the roast chicken, eggs, tomatoes, avocados, spring onions (scallions) and lettuce. Mix the ingredients in a bowl with the crisp bacon and cress, then tumble onto a large plate and serve with the creamy dressing alongside to drizzle over.

<h3>POACHED EGG &</h3>

★

CONGEE RICE

This is a cleansing bowl of comfort. The rice is cooked
to a soft, creamy porridge and the poached egg
adds a glorious richness.

  SERVES 2

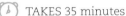 TAKES 35 minutes

3 spring onions (scallions)
3cm/1¼ inch piece root ginger,
    peeled
2 garlic cloves
1 tbsp groundnut oil
120g/4oz jasmine rice
80ml/2½fl oz Shaoxing rice wine
1 litre/1 quart hot vegetable stock
1½ tbsp soy sauce
1 tbsp Chinese rice wine vinegar
140g/5oz shredded spring greens
2 eggs
salt and freshly ground
    black pepper
To serve
pinch of chilli flakes (red pepper
    flakes)
handful roasted unsalted peanuts,
    roughly chopped
small handful coriander (cilantro)
    leaves
1 lime, cut into wedges

Whizz the spring onions (scallions), ginger and
garlic in a food processor until finely chopped (or
chop by hand). Heat the oil in a large pan, add the
ginger and spring onion mix and fry for a couple of
minutes over medium heat. Stir through the rice,
then pour in the rice wine and let it bubble for 1–2
minutes, until reduced a little. Pour in the stock,
soy sauce and rice vinegar and gently simmer for 25
minutes, stirring now and then. At the 20-minute
mark, stir through the shredded greens to wilt. The
rice should be really soft and the stock thickened
and soupy. Taste to check the seasoning.

Meanwhile, poach your eggs by filling a pan up to
about 5cm/2 inches with water and bring to the
boil. Reduce the heat right down to a shudder. In
turn, crack each egg into a teacup and gently slide
it into the water, at separate sides of the pan. Cook
for 2½ minutes, or until the whites have set.

Spoon the congee between warmed bowls and top
each with a poached egg, a pinch of chilli flakes
(red pepper flakes), roasted peanuts and a few
coriander (cilantro) leaves. Serve with lime wedges
to squeeze.

SPICED

★

HASH

Hash is pretty adaptable and it's a fabulous way to use up leftovers – a handful of kale, some chopped sausages and of course that half-empty box of eggs.

 SERVES 2 generously

🕐 TAKES 40 minutes

1 tbsp rapeseed oil
knob of butter
550g/1¼lb Desiree potatoes,
    peeled and cut into 2cm/
    ¾ inch cubes
½ tsp turmeric
1 tsp cumin
100g/3½oz salt beef, chopped
55g/2oz spring cabbage, shredded
4 spring onions (scallions), finely
    sliced
4 eggs
handful flat-leaf parsley,
    finely chopped
1 small red chilli pepper, finely
    sliced
brown sauce, to serve
salt and freshly ground
    black pepper

Heat the oil and butter in a large frying pan. Add the cubed potatoes in a single layer, season well and fry over medium heat for 20 minutes, stirring occasionally. Stir through the spices and continue to fry for 2 minutes, then add the salt beef and cook for a further 3 minutes, or until the potato is golden, crisped and cooked through.

Meanwhile, bring a pan of salted water to the boil. Add the shredded cabbage and cook for 2–3 minutes. Drain, pat dry with kitchen paper then add to the frying pan and fold through, along with the spring onions (scallions).

Make four depressions in the mixture and crack your eggs into these. Season and cook over low heat for 12 minutes, or until the whites are set. Finish with a scattering of parsley and chilli, and serve with brown sauce.

TWICE-BAKED
★
CRAB SOUFFLÉS

'Twice-baked' takes all the stress out of a soufflé. Make in advance then turn out and reheat to serve.

🍴 SERVES 4

⏰ TAKES 50 minutes, plus cooling

35g/1¼oz butter, plus extra
   to grease
35g/1¼oz plain (all-purpose) flour
170ml/6fl oz full-fat (whole) milk
½ tsp mustard powder
grated zest of 1 lemon
1 small red chilli pepper, deseeded
   and finely diced
80g/3oz finely grated Gruyère
100g/3½oz fresh white and
   brown crabmeat
3 eggs, separated
2 heaped tbsp chopped dill and
   chives, plus extra to garnish
4 tbsp crème fraîche
salt and freshly ground
   black pepper

Grease four 200ml/7fl oz dariole moulds or ramekins with butter. Preheat the oven to 180°C/350°F/gas 4.

Melt the butter in a small pan over medium heat, add the flour and whisk to form a paste. Cook for 1 minute, then gradually add the milk, whisking so as to avoid lumps. Bring the mixture to the boil and let it bubble for a minute until thickened. Remove from the heat. Spoon into a bowl and stir through the mustard powder, lemon zest, chilli, 55g/2oz of the cheese and seasoning. Allow to cool, then stir through the crabmeat, egg yolks and herbs.

In a clean bowl, whisk the egg whites to stiff peaks. Stir a little of the whites through the crab mixture to loosen, then carefully fold through the rest.

Spoon between the prepared dariole moulds and place in a roasting tin. Pour enough just-boiled water into the tin to come halfway up the sides of the moulds. Transfer to the oven and cook for 20 minutes. Remove and set aside to cool. Increase the oven temperature to 220°C/430°F/gas 8.

Run a knife around the edge of each soufflé and turn out into an ovenproof dish. In a small bowl, mix the crème fraîche and the remaining 30g/1oz Gruyère with a little salt and pepper. Place a spoonful on top of each soufflé and bake for 10 minutes. Serve garnished with herbs.

DESSERTS &

★

DRINKS

PANETTONE
★
PAIN PERDU

Pain Perdu is best made with an enriched bread like brioche or, as in this case, panettone. Traditionally, it is made with slightly stale bread, which helps to soak up more of the egg batter.

 SERVES 4

 TAKES 10 minutes

200g/7oz strawberries, hulled
    and cut in half
2 tbsp golden caster (superfine)
    sugar
150g/5½oz raspberries
3 eggs
100ml/3½fl oz full-fat (whole) milk
4 thick slices leftover panettone,
    at least a day old
20g/¾oz butter
icing (confectioner's) sugar, to dust
maple syrup or honey, to drizzle
mascarpone, to serve

Place the strawberries in a small pan with the sugar and heat gently until the sugar has dissolved. Stir through the raspberries and continue to cook for a couple of minutes, until they start to release their juices. Remove and set aside.

Mix the eggs and milk together in a shallow bowl, and soak two panettone slices on each side. Heat half the butter in a large frying pan, add the soaked panettone and fry over medium heat for 2 minutes on each side, until golden and crisped. Remove and dust with icing (confectioner's) sugar. Repeat the soaking and frying with the remaining two slices of panettone.

Place a slice of panettone on each plate, spoon the syrupy berries over the top, drizzle with the maple syrup and serve with mascarpone.

MANGO & LIME

ETON MESS

Eton mess is such a crowd-pleasing dessert: a luxurious sticky mess of broken meringue, whipped cream and, in this case, juicy, honeyed mango.

 SERVES 4

 TAKES 15 minutes

2 ripe mangoes
juice and zest of 1 lime
2 tbsp runny honey
1 cardamom pod, seeds removed
   and crushed
250ml/8fl oz double (heavy) cream
4 tsp icing (confectioner's) sugar
4 meringues (see page 151)
few bright-green slivered
   pistachios, to garnish
few small mint leaves, to garnish

Peel the mangoes, cut the flesh away from the stones and chop. Place three-quarters of the mango flesh in a bowl and add half the lime juice and all of the zest. In a food processor, blitz the remaining mango and lime juice with the honey, crushed cardamom seeds and 1 tablespoon of water to a smooth purée.

Whip the cream and icing (confectioner's) sugar in a bowl to form soft peaks. Break the meringues into chunky pieces and fold through the cream along with the mango purée. Spoon between four bowls, add the chopped mango and scatter with the pistachios and mint leaves.

ÎLES

★

FLOTTANTES

You can add some toasted chopped nuts or shattered pieces
of praline instead of caramel, if you like.

 SERVES 4

 TAKES 30 minutes,
plus cooling

For the custard
240ml/8fl oz full-fat (whole) milk
½ vanilla pod, cut in half
    lengthways and seeds scraped
2 large eggs, separated
125g/4½oz caster (superfine) sugar
pinch of sea salt
For the caramel
100g/3½oz caster (superfine) sugar

Make the custard. Bring the milk, vanilla pod and
seeds almost to the boil in a small pan – you will
see bubbles appearing on the surface. Remove and
allow to cool briefly.

In a bowl, whisk the egg yolks and 40g/1½oz of the
sugar. Slowly pour in the warm milk, whisking well,
then pour the mixture into a clean pan. Heat gently,
stirring constantly until the custard coats the back
of a wooden spoon. Pour through a sieve into a jug
and leave to cool, covered with cling film.

To make the caramel, put the sugar and 100ml/
3½fl oz water into a small pan and bring slowly to
a simmer. Once the sugar has melted, let it bubble
until it becomes copper in colour. Remove from
the heat and set aside (this can be reheated).

Half-fill a pan with water and bring to the boil.
Whisk the egg whites with the salt to form stiff
peaks, then add the 85g/3oz of sugar, a tablespoon
at a time, whisking to stiff peaks with each addition.
Turn down the heat until the water is barely
simmering and, using two large spoons, gently slide
about quarter of the mixture onto the surface of
the water, teasing the top into peaks. Cook two
'islands' at a time for 2½ minutes. Lift out with a
slotted spoon and drain on kitchen paper. To serve,
divide the custard between four bowls. Pop a
meringue on top and finish with warm caramel.

SOUFFLÉD APPLE & RASPBERRY ★ OMELETTE

Light as a cloud, sweet and spiked with sharp apples and raspberries, this can be served for pudding or breakfast.

 SERVES 4

TAKES 25 minutes

2 large Cox or Braeburn apples
1 tbsp lemon juice
40g/1½oz butter
1½ tbsp caster (superfine) sugar
1 tsp ground cinnamon
4 eggs, separated
80g/3oz icing (confectioner's) sugar, plus extra to dust
80g/3oz raspberries
runny honey, to drizzle

Peel the apples, remove the cores and cut each into 12 wedges. Toss the apple wedges in a bowl with lemon juice to stop them browning. Set aside.

Heat 30g/1oz of the butter in a 26cm/10¼ inch non-stick frying pan. Add the apple slices in a single layer and fry over medium-low heat for 7–8 minutes, until golden and softened. Sprinkle with the sugar and cinnamon, and continue to cook for a further minute, until the apples are caramelised. Remove to a plate and wipe the pan clean.

Whisk the egg yolks with the icing (confectioner's) sugar, until thick and creamy. Using a clean whisk and a clean bowl, whisk the egg whites to form stiff peaks then fold through the egg yolk-sugar mixture, taking care not to knock out too much air.

Preheat the grill to medium-high. Melt the remaining butter in the pan. Once the butter begins to foam, add the whisked eggs, smooth the surface and scatter over the apples and raspberries. Cook over low heat for 3½ minutes, until the underside is golden. Place the pan under the grill and cook for 3 minutes, or until golden and puffed – the inside should still be soft. Dust with icing sugar, drizzle over the honey and serve immediately.

PORTUGUESE
★
CUSTARD TARTS

These custard tarts have a crisp pastry shell and
wobbly vanilla centre. They are a little time-consuming
but worth it, nonetheless.

 MAKES 10

 TAKES 1 hour, plus
cooling

325g/11½oz golden caster
(superfine) sugar
pared zest of 1 lemon
325ml/11½fl oz full-fat (whole)
milk
1 cinnamon stick
40g/1½oz cornflour (cornstarch),
plus extra to dust
4 large egg yolks
1 tsp vanilla extract
butter, to grease
300g/10½oz all-butter puff pastry

In a small pan, combine 200g/7oz of the sugar, the
lemon zest and 200ml/7fl oz water and place over
medium heat, stirring to dissolve the sugar. Bring
to the boil for 6 minutes to reach 108°C/226°F on a
thermometer (or until a little dropped into a bowl
of cold water forms a thin thread). Remove from
the heat and cool before discarding the peel.

Heat the milk and cinnamon in a clean pan over
medium heat to warm through. In a small bowl,
whisk the cornflour (cornstarch) with a little of the
warm milk to form a paste. Bring the milk to the
boil then whisk in the flour paste, stirring for
3 minutes until thickened. Pour into a bowl and
set aside.

In another bowl, whisk the egg yolks, the remaining
sugar and vanilla extract, then slowly pour this over
the thickened milk, whisking as you do so.

method continues overleaf...

★ ★ ★ ★ ★ ★ ★ ★ ★ ★ ★ ★ ★ ★ ★

★ ★

PORTUGUESE CUSTARD TARTS

continued...

Strain the mixture through a sieve into a bowl, to remove any lumps, then set aside to cool. Cover in cling film and chill. Once cold, stir through the cooled sugar syrup. Grease 10 holes of a 12-hole muffin tin generously with butter and chill.

Roll the pastry out into a long rectangle of about 40 x 18cm/16 x 7 inch, and roll up from the short end into a tight log. Cut into 10 x 1.5cm/4 x ½ inch rounds (discarding the ends) and roll each out into a 10cm/4 inch disc. Use these to line your muffin tin and chill until needed.

Preheat the oven to 250°C/480°F/gas 9 and place a baking sheet inside. Divide the custard between the pastry cases (leaving a 1cm/½ inch gap between the top of the filling and the pastry). Transfer to the preheated baking tray and bake for 18–20 minutes, until the pastry is crisp and the custard just set. Remove from the oven and leave for 5 minutes then carefully loosen with a knife and cool completely on a wire rack.

ORANGE CUSTARD
★
MERINGUE & RHUBARB

This recipe makes double the amount of crisp, chewy meringues needed. Simply use what's left for the Mango and Lime Eton Mess on page 142. All the elements in this can be made in advance, making it the ideal throw-together pud.

 SERVES 4

 TAKES 1 hour 45 minutes, plus cooling

For the meringues (makes 8)
3 large egg whites
175g/6oz caster (superfine) sugar
For the rhubarb
400g/14oz rhubarb, cut into
   5cm/2 inch pieces
zest and juice of 1 orange
125g/4½oz caster (superfine) sugar
For the orange custard
240ml/8fl oz full-fat (whole) milk
½ vanilla pod, cut in half
   lengthways and seeds scraped
2 large egg yolks
40g/1½oz caster (superfine) sugar
finely grated zest of ½ orange and
   1 tbsp juice

Preheat the oven to 140°C/275°F/gas 1 and line two baking sheets with baking parchment.

Make the meringues by whisking the egg whites in a clean bowl to form stiff peaks. Start adding the sugar, a spoonful at a time, whisking back up to stiff peaks between each addition. Spoon eight pillowy mounds onto the lined trays, leaving a good gap between each. Make a dip in the top of each. Bake for 50 minutes, until the meringues easily peel away from the paper. Turn off the oven, leaving them inside to cool completely. Store four meringues away in an airtight container.

Preheat the oven to 160°C/320°F/gas 2. Arrange the rhubarb in a shallow roasting tray with the orange zest and juice and the sugar. Roast for 45 minutes, or until tender, then transfer to a dish and pour over any juices from the tray. Set aside to cool.

method continues overleaf...

★ ★ ★ ★ ★ ★ ★ ★ ★ ★ ★ ★ ★ ★ ★ ★

★ ★

ORANGE CUSTARD, MERINGUE & RHUBARB
continued...

For the custard, bring the milk, vanilla pod and seeds almost to the boil in a small pan – you will see bubbles appearing on the surface. Remove and allow to cool briefly.

In a bowl, mix the egg yolks and sugar together, then slowly pour over the warm milk. Pour the mixture into a clean pan and heat gently, stirring until the custard is thick enough to coat the back of a wooden spoon. Pour through a sieve into a bowl and stir through the orange zest and juice. Set aside to cool, covered with cling film (plastic wrap).

Serve the meringues in shallow bowls with the roasted rhubarb, their juices and the orange custard spooned over the top.

CHOCOLATE CHERRY
★
CLAFOUTIS

Clafoutis is a simple batter pudding. Here, I've added chocolate, which goes beautifully with cherries, but you can change the fruit according to what's in season.

 SERVES 2

 TAKES 45 minutes,
plus macerating

200g/7oz cherries, pitted
55g/2oz jarred black cherries
   in kirsch
1½ tbsp kirsch
50g/1¾oz caster (superfine) sugar
10g melted butter, plus extra
   to grease
demerara sugar, to sprinkle
1 large egg, plus 1 large egg yolk
pinch of fine sea salt
25g/¾oz plain (all-purpose) flour
1 tbsp dark cocoa powder
140ml/5fl oz Jersey or regular
   full-fat (whole) milk
25g/¾oz finely chopped dark
   chocolate (70% cocoa solids)
icing (confectioner's) sugar, to dust
crème fraîche, to serve

Squeeze the cherries a little to burst their skins and put in a dish with the jarred cherries, kirsch and 20g (¾oz) of the caster (superfine) sugar. Set aside for 1 hour to macerate, stirring occasionally.

Preheat oven to 200°C/400°F/gas 6. Grease the inside of a 20cm/8 inch ovenproof dish with butter and sprinkle with demerara sugar.

Whisk the egg, yolk, remaining caster sugar and the salt together in a bowl for 5 minutes, until pale and thickened. In separate bowl, mix the flour and cocoa together, then sift over the egg mixture and fold through. Add the milk, melted butter, chopped chocolate, macerated cherries and their juices, and gently fold in.

Pour into the buttered dish and bake for 25–30 minutes, or until golden and firm on top. Dust with icing (confectioner's) sugar and serve warm with crème fraîche.

CRÈME
★
CARAMEL

These quivering baked custards are bathed in a sweet caramel sauce. You can easily make these a day ahead and enjoy them the next day.

 SERVES 4

TAKES 1 hour 15 minutes, plus chilling

340ml/11fl oz full-fat (whole) milk
1 vanilla pod, split in half
   lengthways and seeds scraped
100g/3½oz soft light brown sugar
butter, to grease
2 eggs, plus 2 egg yolks
65g/2¼oz caster (superfine) sugar

Preheat the oven to 150°C/300°F/gas 2. Pour the milk into a pan, add the vanilla pod and seeds and bring almost to the boil. Remove from the heat as soon as bubbles appear on the surface and set aside to infuse while you make the caramel.

Warm four 150ml/5fl oz ramekins in a low oven.

Spoon the brown sugar into a pan with 90ml/3fl oz water and place over low heat until the sugar has dissolved. Let the mixture bubble until it is a dark caramel colour. Drop a tiny amount of the syrup on a plate to check if it hardens. Immediately divide the syrup between the warmed ramekins, swirling to cover the base, and then set aside to harden. Then butter the sides of the ramekins.

Whisk the eggs, yolks and caster (superfine) sugar together in a bowl. Pour over the vanilla-infused milk, whisking, then strain into a jug and divide between the ramekins. Arrange in a small roasting tin and carefully fill the tin with just-boiled water to reach halfway up the sides of the ramekins. Cover each with foil and cook in the oven for 25 minutes, then remove the foil and continue to cook for 25 more minutes, or until the custard has just set. Allow to cool and invert onto plates to serve.

SALTED CARAMEL

★

CHOCOLATE SOUFFLES

No one is going to argue with this fluffy combination of
chocolate and salted caramel. A dream in a dish.

 SERVES 4

 TAKES 30 minutes

a little melted butter, to grease
120g/4¼oz dark chocolate (70%
   cocoa solids), broken into small
   pieces
2 tbsp double (heavy) cream
3 large eggs, separated
35g/1¼oz caster (superfine) sugar
   plus extra to dust
icing (confectioner's) sugar, to dust
For the sauce
120g/4¼oz sugar
55g/2oz butter, cubed
4 tbsp double (heavy) cream
1 tsp sea salt

Preheat the oven to 220°C/430°F/gas 8 and put
a baking sheet inside. Brush the insides of four
150ml/5fl oz ramekins with melted butter, sprinkle
with caster (superfine) sugar and tip out the excess.

Make the sauce. Place the sugar and 100ml/3½fl
oz water in a small pan over low heat, stirring until
the sugar has dissolved. Increase the heat and let
the mixture bubble until it is a rich caramel colour.
Add the cubed butter, stir to melt, then pour in the
cream and stir through the salt. Set to one side and
gently reheat when ready to serve.

Melt the chocolate with the cream in a heatproof
bowl set over a pan of barely simmering water
(the bowl should not touch the water). Remove
from the heat and stir through the egg yolks. In
a separate, scrupulously clean bowl, whisk the
egg whites to form firm peaks. Add the 35g/1¼oz
of sugar a spoonful at a time, whisking between
each addition. Stir a spoonful of the whites into
the chocolate mixture to loosen up the mix, then
carefully fold in the rest.

Divide the mixture between the ramekins. Run a
knife over the top to level, wipe the rims and run
a clean fingertip around the edges. Pop onto the
preheated baking sheet and turn the temperature
down to 200°C/400°F/gas 6. Bake for 10 minutes
until risen with a very slight wobble in the centre.

CHOCOLATEY

★

CUSTARD TART

Chocolate pastry works well with this classic custard filling,
which is gloriously silky and wobbly.

 SERVES 8

 TAKES 1 hour 20 minutes,
plus chilling

For the pastry
175g/6¼oz plain (all-purpose) flour
1 tbsp cocoa, plus extra to dust
50g/1¾oz icing (confectioner's)
   sugar
pinch of sea salt
100g/3½oz cold butter, cubed
1 egg, separated

For the custard filling
550ml/18½fl oz whipping cream
1 vanilla pod, split in half
   lengthways and seeds scraped
2 large eggs, plus 2 egg yolks
100g/3½oz golden caster
   (superfine) sugar
freshly grated nutmeg

Whizz the flour, cocoa, icing (confectioner's) sugar and salt in a food processor. Add the butter and pulse to fine breadcrumbs. Mix the egg yolk with 1 tbsp iced water, then pour into the food processor whilst pulsing. The mixture should form a dough. Bring together into a flat disc with your hands. Wrap in cling film and chill for 30 minutes. Roll out to line a 20cm/8 inch loose-bottomed tart tin. Prick the base with a fork and chill for 20 minutes.

Preheat the oven to 200°C/400°F/gas 6, and put a baking sheet inside to heat up. Line the tart with baking parchment and baking beans, and place on the hot baking sheet. Bake for 15 minutes, then remove the paper and beans and return to the oven for 5 minutes. Brush the inside with a little whisked egg white and cook for 2 minutes. Remove and turn the oven down to 160°C/320°F/gas 2.

Bring the cream, vanilla pod and seeds almost to the boil in a small pan – you will see bubbles appearing. Remove and allow to cool briefly.

Mix the eggs, yolks and sugar together in a bowl. Slowly pour over the vanilla cream, whisking, then strain through a sieve into a jug. Carefully pour into the pastry case and grate nutmeg over the surface. Bake for 40 minutes, or until just set. Remove and leave for 10 minutes in the tin before dusting with cocoa. Serve warm or at room temperature.

CLASSIC

★

ZABAGLIONE

A truly delicious, light foamy Italian dessert, zabaglione is made with fortified wine. Like custard, the eggs need to be cooked over a very gentle heat, just enough for the mixture to thicken and swell – take care not to overheat otherwise it will curdle.

 SERVES 4

 TAKES 20 minutes

5 large egg yolks
seeds from 1 vanilla pod
100g/3½oz golden caster (superfine) sugar
pinch of ground cinnamon
75ml/4½ tbsp marsala or Madeira wine
4 Amaretti biscuits, roughly crushed

Put the egg yolks, vanilla seeds and sugar into a large heatproof bowl. Using an electric handheld beater, whisk for 4 minutes, or until the mixture is pale, thick and creamy. Mix in the cinnamon.

Place the bowl over a pan of barely simmering water (the bowl should not touch the water). Slowly add the marsala, whisking all the time. Continue to whisk for 6 minutes or so, until the mixture thickens and swells enough to leave a trail when the beaters are lifted. Remove from heat and immediately spoon between four glasses. Sprinkle with crushed Amaretti biscuits and serve.

LEMON

CURD

Home-made lemon curd is a world apart from the shop-bought stuff. Serve it with pancakes to add a sweet sharp kick, lather onto soft white bread or toast, or fold through whipped cream for a no-fuss dessert. There are many lovely recipes that would benefit from a good dollop of this sunshine spread.

 MAKES 2 × 370g jars

 TAKES 15 minutes, plus cooling

140g/5oz butter, cut into cubes
230g/8oz golden caster (superfine) sugar
zest of 3 large unwaxed lemons, plus juice of 4 lemons (about 180ml/6fl oz)
4 large eggs

Put the butter, sugar, lemon zest and juice into a large heatproof bowl set over a pan of barely simmering water (the bowl should not touch the water). Allow the butter to melt gently.

Lightly whisk the eggs then add to the lemon mixture and cook for 10–12 minutes, watching closely and whisking now and then, until the mixture thickens enough to coat the back of a wooden spoon.

Remove from the heat and allow to cool, stirring occasionally every now and then. When completely cooled, pour between two sterilised jars and store in the fridge for up to 2 weeks.

PISCO

★

SOUR

Egg white-only cocktails give a silky, foamy texture and a
glorious frothy top. Pisco is a grape brandy and
best showcased in the Pisco Sour, a favourite of
mine and I'm sure soon to be yours.

 SERVES 2

 TAKES 5 minutes

100ml/3½fl oz pisco
100ml/3½fl oz lime juice (about 5
   limes)
50ml/1¾fl oz sugar syrup
1 large egg white
dash of Angostura bitters

Measure all the ingredients except the bitters into
a cocktail shaker. Shake vigorously for 20 seconds
then strain into two glasses. Add 3 drops of bitters
into each glass through the foamy top and serve.

ADVOCAAT &

★

SNOWBALL

Home-made advocaat is seriously good. Made from eggs, sugar and brandy, it is rich, creamy and warming, a very different 'bottle of eggs' to the commercial variety. Pour it over ice cream, fold through whipped cream, simply serve over ice, or for a taste of Christmas shake up in a snowball.

MAKES 800ml advocaat and 1 snowball

TAKES 15 minutes, plus cooling (advocaat), 2 minutes (snowball)

For the advocaat
9 large egg yolks
225g/8oz golden caster (superfine) sugar
seeds from 2 vanilla pods
360ml/12fl oz brandy
For the snowball
50ml/1¾oz advocaat
juice of ½ lime
ice cubes
100ml/3½fl oz lemonade
grated nutmeg, to dust
maraschino cherry, to serve

To make the advocaat, use a handheld electric beater to mix the egg yolks, sugar and vanilla seeds in a large heatproof bowl for 3 minutes, or until pale, thickened and a trail is left when the beaters are lifted. Gradually add the brandy, beating well.

Place the bowl over a pan of barely simmering water (make sure the bowl does not touch the water) and heat gently for about 5 minutes, stirring constantly with a wooden spoon, until the mixture has thickened further and really coats the back of your spoon. Poor into a jug and leave to cool before storing in a sterilised sealed bottle in the fridge. Shake the bottle before using.

To make the snowball, mix the advocaat, lime juice and a handful of ice in a cocktail shaker. Pour into a highball glass and top up with lemonade. Dust with a little grated nutmeg and pop a maraschino cherry on top to serve.

NEGRONI

FLIP

A 'flip' is a shaken whole-egg cocktail; it is fluffy, creamy and weighty. Here, a classic negroni is given a makeover.

 SERVES 2

 TAKES 2 minutes

30ml/2 tbsp gin
30ml/2 tbsp Campari
30ml/2 tbsp sweet vermouth, such
   as Martini Rosso
2 tsp sugar syrup
1 large egg
ice cubes
2 thin orange slices, to garnish

Measure the spirits and the sugar syrup into a cocktail shaker. Add the egg along with a handful of ice. Shake furiously for 20 seconds. Strain into two glasses and garnish with a slice of orange.

INDEX

★★★★★★★★★★★★★★★★★★★★★★★★★★★★★★★★★★★★★